SEX

WHAT THE CATHOLIC CHURCH TEACHES

JOHN REDFORD

SEX
What the Catholic Church Teaches

The alternative to moral anarchy

ST PAULS

The versions of the Scriptures used throughout this book are either the Revised Standard Version (marked RSV) or the New Revised Standard Version, (Catholic Edition).

ST PAULS Publishing
187 Battersea Bridge Road, London SW11 3AS, UK

Copyright © ST PAULS 2000

ISBN 085439 599 7

Set by TuKan, Fareham, Hampshire, UK
Produced in the EC
Printed by The Guernsey Press Co. Ltd., Guernsey, C.I.

ST PAULS is an activity of the priests and brothers
of the Society of St Paul who proclaim the Gospel
through the media of social communication

Like other people, they (Christians) marry and beget children, though they do not expose their infants. Any Christian is free to share his neighbour's table, but never his marriage bed.

Letter from Diognetus; a letter dating from 200 to 300 AD written by an unknown Christian to an unknown enquirer

Contents

Introduction

We are living in a seducing society. The media, the forces of big business, even sometimes the governments of the world, are encouraging the trivialisation of sex at every moment of our lives. Sex is a billion-dollar industry; and the more sex, the more money will be made by many people.

One organisation in the world stands out above the rest in protest against this cheapening of sex: the Catholic Church. This is because the Church, following the teaching of Jesus our Founder, considers sex a sacred and valuable human activity, a sign of the fullness of love between a married couple. That is why the Church values marriage as a sacrament, and limits sex to those male and female couples who are married. And that is why the Church encourages some to give up sex altogether, and to take vows of chastity. The reason is the value which is placed upon the sex act. It is not for pure pleasure, only as a means of personal physical communion between those committed to each other for life in marriage.

That is also why the Catholic Church is attacked in particular on this matter of sex today. The Catholic Church is frequently discriminated against in the media. The Church is rarely allowed to present its position. Rather, where there is a controversial question in Catholic sexual ethics or in bioethics, a representative of the Church is hardly ever invited to present the Church's own teaching. Rather, a Catholic who dissents from the Church's teaching is wheeled in for an opinion. Every society or organisation has dissenters from its official position. They have a right to express their opinion, of course. But every other organisation seems to be given the right to express its official position. That never seems to happen where the Catholic Church is concerned, perhaps the largest organisation in the world with more than a billion members. People are just not allowed to hear the Church speak for itself. That means that, even within the membership of the Catholic Church, the Church's own position is obscured by the continuous propaganda of the media and of the pressurising forces in society.

This book is an attempt to put the Catholic Church's own position by one who believes that it is right. Indeed, what I am arguing in these pages would have been agreed by all Christian denominations at the beginning of this century. I know also that our Moslem and Jewish friends will also agree with much if not the majority of what is written here. It is not my personal opinion, although it is expressed personally. It represents the voice of human as well as religious tradition.

My literary style throughout this book will be the form of question and answer; a kind of extended interview. This style has its roots in the scholastic era of theology, from the eleventh and twelfth centuries onwards, the cradle of our present university education system, where objections were raised to a particular view (e.g. 'It seems that God does not exist') and the objections were then answered (e.g. with reasons for God's existence). The objections raised the interest of the student, and challenged the lecturer to stay on the ball. The modern equivalent is the TV interview, where the star TV personality represents the public putting objections to the politician, thus trying (often vainly) to force the politician to give a straight answer for the public benefit. Here I have no interest in giving 'political' answers, because I really do believe that the Church is the 'pillar and bulwark of the truth' (1 Tim 3:15), from divine revelation giving us the truth about our sexuality as about our humanity.

Your first question will no doubt be 'What do you, a celibate priest, know about sex? Surely, someone who is married ought to be writing about sex, from personal experience!'

This seems to be a fair question; but is it when you think more about it? We will forget the fact that many marriages today are breaking up, and so perhaps married people are not always themselves a good advertisement for marriage. But that is not fair, either. Thousands, millions of marriages are still happy and faithful. Much more important is what a happily married couple said to me recently. 'Father, we are authorities on marriage, *our* marriage'. They have made a good point. Just because they are married does not make them authorities on everyone else's marriage.

But there is still an even more important point. If I may put it a little crudely, married people are not the only human beings with sexual organs. We are all sexual beings. We all came from the womb of our mothers, and most of us suckled her breasts. The beauty of this experience is very important psychologically in the growth of a child.

This came home to me recently as I visited a young couple who had just moved into their new home with a new baby. As we sat in the front room, the mother quite unselfconsciously began to feed her child at the breast. The little baby made cooing sounds of satisfaction. No wealthy man feeding on his caviar in an expensive restaurant would have had a fraction of the enjoyment which that young baby had. Psychologists tell us how important childhood experiences are. The experience of a mother's love through breastfeeding is one of deep love, not just of feeding as such, which makes the baby secure and happy in the early months of growth.

The Bible uses the image of the child at the breast of its

11

mother as an image of trust in God our Creator: 'But I have calmed and quieted my soul, like a wearied child with its mother; my soul is like the wearied child that is with me' (Ps 131:2).

God, therefore, has made us sexual beings, male and female as the *Catechism of the Catholic Church* says most beautifully:

'Male and female God created them...'

2331 'God is love and in himself he lives a mystery of personal loving communion. Creating the human race in his own image ... God inscribed in the humanity of man and woman the *vocation*, and thus the capacity and responsibility, *of love* and communion."

'God created man in his own image ... male and female he created them'; He blessed them and said, 'Be fruitful and multiply'; 'When God created man, he made him in the likeness of God. Male and female he created them, and he blessed them and named them Man when they were created.'

2332 *Sexuality* affects all aspects of the human person in the unity of his body and soul. It especially concerns affectivity, the capacity to love and to procreate, and in a more general way the aptitude for forming bonds of communion with others.

2333 Everyone, man and woman, should acknowledge and accept his sexual *identity*. Physical, moral and spiritual *difference* and *complementarity* are oriented toward the goods of marriage and the flourishing of family life. The harmony of the couple and of society depends in part on the way in which the complementarity, needs and mutual support between the sexes are lived out.

What the Catechism is saying is clear. We are all sexual beings, whether we are young or old, married or single, and whatever our sexual orientation might be. Sex is ordained by God for the procreation of the human race through married love. But, whether a particular human being is married or unmarried, every person is called to form bonds of communion with others. In this way, married people can help those who are single, widowed or divorced, and vice versa; not to say, of course, the young. But we all must grow in our understanding of our sexual identity, in order to understand ourselves as people. And every human being has a role to play, something to offer the community.

Celibate priests all have to come to terms with their sexuality over a long length of time. Temptations will always be there, as long as we are alive and virile. The story goes of a young curate after a difficult night of temptation from 'impure thoughts' asking his parish priest at breakfast, 'Father, when do temptations to impurity go away?' The older priest replied, 'After about sixty.' Next morning, the parish priest came down and said to his curate ruefully, 'You know yesterday I said that temptations to purity end at about the age of sixty? Well, make that sixty-one.'

To attain mastery of oneself, body and soul is a lifetime process. But at least I can say that I am not only by the grace of God a celibate priest: I am also a happy one. The journey, the hard work, is worth it. Married couples who have remained faithful to their calling will say the same. Celibate chastity has to be worked at, just as does married chastity. If the sexual revolution of the past thirty years has taught us anything at all positive, it is that to get married is not the final solution to problems of chastity. The number of marriage breakdowns would seem to make that a demonstrable fact. The way to happiness is true chastity, whether married or unmarried, because thereby we become masters of ourselves, as the *Catechism of the Catholic Church* says:

2339 Chastity includes an *apprenticeship in self-mastery* which is a training in human freedom. The alternative is clear: either man governs his passions and finds peace, or he lets himself be dominated by them and becomes unhappy.

In our journey through life, we have the greatest help possible, from Christ our High Priest: 'For we do not have a high priest who is unable to sympathise with our weaknesses, but we have one who in every respect has been tested as we are, yet without sin. Let us therefore approach the throne of grace with boldness, so that we may receive mercy and find grace to help in time of need' (Heb 4:15-16).

You will notice how much I quote both Scripture and the *Catechism of the Catholic Church* (referenced by paragraph) in this book. Catholic Faith and teaching is based upon the Bible, the written Word of God, and on Tradition, the teaching and living of the Church throughout the centuries. The new Catechism was first published in 1992 as an Apostolic Constitution by the present pope, John Paul II. It is designed to present comprehensively the Tradition of the Church, and does so in a superb way, not least in the area of sexual ethics.

At the end of the day, I am not just giving my own views or my own experience, except on occasion, where I use the author's privilege! Rather, for all my life as a Catholic, I have accepted and tried to live the teaching of the Church, however imperfectly. And my first aim is to present that teaching, for your consideration.

As Paul said to the Thessalonian Christians: 'We also constantly give thanks to God for this, that when you received the word of God that you heard from us, you accepted it not as a human word but as what it really is, God's word, which is also at work in you believers' (1 Thess 2:13).

Amen!

1

Sex is beautiful

Q. The Catholic Church is against sex, we all know!

A. On the contrary, the Church's teaching is based upon what God has told us in the Word of God written and unwritten. In the Creation story in Genesis, we are told that God made us as human beings both male and female, in his own image. He wanted us to procreate, to rule the earth. He wanted us to have sex! That was part of the divine plan:

> Then God said, 'Let us make humankind in our image, according to our likeness; and let them have dominion over the fish of the sea, and over the birds of the air, and over the cattle, and over all the wild animals of the earth, and over every creeping thing that creeps upon the earth.' So God created humankind in his image, in the image of God he created them; male and female he created them. God blessed them and God said to them, 'Be fruitful and multiply, and fill the earth and subdue it; and have dominion over the fish of the sea and over the birds of the air and over every living thing that moves upon the earth.'
>
> Genesis 1:26-28

Q. But doesn't the Church teach that sex went all wrong with Adam and Eve?

A. Not until after the Fall. Sex is a beautiful concept in the Bible. Genesis tells a primitive story using picture language. It is not a scientific description of the creation of man and woman. But it tells a profound truth:

> So the LORD God caused a deep sleep to fall upon the man, and he slept; then he took one of his ribs and closed up its place with flesh. And the rib that the LORD God had taken from the man he made into a woman and brought her to the man. Then the man said, 'This at last is bone of my bones and flesh of my flesh; this one shall be called Woman, for out of Man this one was taken.' Therefore a man leaves his father and his mother and clings to his wife, and they become one flesh. And the man and his wife were both naked, and were not ashamed.
>
> Genesis 2:21-25

Before our first parents disobeyed God, they were not ashamed of their nakedness, but embraced each other as man and wife, to become 'one flesh', that is one person through bodily union. How beautiful that description is in the Bible! The shame of Adam and Eve's nakedness came later, after they had disobeyed God and eaten from fruit of the forbidden tree (Gen 3:7). Their sin was not sex, because they had sex before they sinned. God accepted that as good, their union to become one flesh.

Their first sin was most likely that of pride.

Q. But the Church teaches that Adam and Eve conceived in sin, does it not?

A. The Church teaches that the consequence of the sin of Adam and Eve is transmitted down the human chain. We will have to deal with the effects of what is called 'Original Sin' later. But again, the Bible teaches that the birth of the first child to Adam and Eve was a beautiful event, just as we see it today in the birth of millions of babies each day: 'Now the man knew his wife Eve, and she conceived and bore Cain, saying, 'I have produced a man with the help of the Lord' (Gen 4:11).

The word 'know' (in Hebrew *yada*) is a lovely way to describe sexual intercourse. We refer in English to 'carnal knowledge', but that sounds cheap. The Hebrew word for 'know' tells us that sex is an intimate form of personal knowledge between man and woman. It is a deep form of communion. And God shares in that act by personally creating a new human being, a child, again made in God's image, with an immortal soul. That is why sex is so beautiful, and so sacred.

Q. But the Church does not teach that we should enjoy sex.

A. On the contrary, the Bible celebrates the enjoyment of sex between two young lovers. The Song of Solomon is a series of love poems, dating from six hundred years BC, in which a young man tells of his burning desire for his beautiful maiden.

> How graceful are your feet in sandals, O queenly
>   maiden!
> Your rounded thighs are like jewels, the work of a
>   master hand.
> Your navel is a rounded bowl that never lacks
>   mixed wine.
> Your belly is a heap of wheat, encircled with lilies.
> Your two breasts are like two fawns, twins
>   of a gazelle.
> Your neck is like an ivory tower.

Your eyes are pools in Heshbon, by the gate
of Bath-rabbim.
Your nose is like a tower of Lebanon, overlooking
Damascus.
Your head crowns you like Carmel, and your flowing
locks are like purple; a king is held captive
in the tresses.
How fair and pleasant you are, O loved one,
delectable maiden!

Song of Solomon 7:1-6

This young man wishes to make love to his young woman.
He longs to kiss her lips and grasp her breasts. Again, the
language is quite explicit, as he sings to his beloved:

You are stately as a palm tree, and your breasts are
like its clusters.
I say I will climb the palm tree and lay hold
of its branches.
Oh, may your breasts be like clusters of the vine, and
the scent of your breath like apples,
and your kisses like the best wine that goes down
smoothly, gliding over lips and teeth.
I am my beloved's, and his desire is for me.
Come, my beloved, let us go forth into the fields,
and lodge in the villages;
let us go out early to the vineyards, and see whether
the vines have budded,
whether the grape blossoms have opened and the
pomegranates are in bloom.
There I will give you my love.
The mandrakes give forth fragrance, and over our
doors are all choice fruits,
new as well as old, which I have laid up for you,
O my beloved.

Song of Solomon 7:7-13

The mandrakes, primitive aphrodisiacs, are blooming, and nothing is going to stop the honeymoon. Is this really the Bible, we might ask? It sounds more like the erotic Sanskrit poetry, the Kamasutra of Vatsyayana! Yes, indeed. Monks, who had most of the Bible read during the day, were not allowed to hear the Song of Solomon read in public, because it might stimulate sexual fantasies for those who were celibate!

The young woman is equally explicit in her praise of her young hero's male anatomy. She is nearly frantic with desire:

I adjure you, O daughters of Jerusalem, if you find
    my beloved,
tell him this: I am faint with love.

What is your beloved more than another beloved,
    O fairest among women?
What is your beloved more than another beloved,
    that you thus adjure us?

My beloved is all radiant and ruddy, distinguished
    among ten thousand
His head is the finest gold; his locks are wavy, black
    as a raven
His eyes are like doves beside springs of water, bathed
    in milk, fitly set.
His cheeks are like beds of spices, yielding fragrance.
His lips are lilies, distilling liquid myrrh.
His arms are rounded gold, set with jewels.
His body is ivory work, encrusted with sapphires.
His legs are alabaster columns, set upon bases of gold,
His appearance is like Lebanon, choice as the cedars.
His speech is most sweet, and he is altogether
    desirable.
This is my beloved and this is my friend, O daughters
    of Jerusalem.

Song of Solomon 5:8-16

This is beautiful erotic poetry ('erotic' as opposed to 'pornographic' – there is a serious difference, as we shall see later). It celebrates the bliss of young love, and the sexual beauty of the human body, the woman's breasts, navel, thighs, lovely hair, the man's powerful muscles, his sexual organs and other protrusions described as 'sapphires', his feet as 'bases of gold'. The pleasure, the love itself, is God-given. In the past, Jewish and Christian commentators have seen it as a type of the spiritual love of God. But Jews and Christians today are rightly seeing it first and foremost in its plain meaning, as a celebration in the Word of God of sexual love.

Q. Why, then, is sin so much associated with sex in Christian tradition?

A. St Augustine said, 'The corruption of the best is the worst' (*Corruptio optimi pessimum est*). The sexual instinct is one of the most intense of all human pleasures. That is why its wrong use can do so much damage. We turn again to the book of Genesis, but this time to a tragic and cruel story, the rape of Dinah.

Dinah was the daughter of the patriarch Jacob by his first wife Leah; Sichem was a young man, son of one Hamor of the Hivites, a local tribe, not one of the twelve tribes of Israel. Sichem forced Dinah to have intercourse with him, but then fell in love with her and wanted to marry her. Sichem's father Hamor went to bargain with the sons of Jacob for a reasonable price for his son to marry Dinah. The young men of the tribe of Jacob were deeply angry with Sichem for such an insult, raping their sister, and determined revenge.

They required Sichem's tribe to become Israelites, and so to be circumcised. But it was all a trick. There were no anaesthetics those days for the operation of circumcision, needless to say! On the third day after they had been circumcised, and were not yet healed, the Israelites struck:

On the third day, when they were still in pain, two of the sons of Jacob, Simeon and Levi, Dinah's brothers, took their swords and came against the city unawares, and killed all the males. They killed Hamor and his son Shechem with the sword, and took Dinah out of Shechem's house, and went away. And the other sons of Jacob came upon the slain, and plundered the city, because their sister had been defiled. They took their flocks and their herds, their donkeys, and whatever was in the city and in the field. All their wealth, all their little ones and their wives, all that was in the houses, they captured and made their prey. Then Jacob said to Simeon and Levi, 'You have brought trouble on me by making me odious to the inhabitants of the land, the Canaanites and the Perizzites; my numbers are few, and if they gather themselves against me and attack me, I shall be destroyed, both I and my household.' But they said, 'Should our sister be treated like a whore?'

Genesis 34:24-31

The Song of Solomon treats of the beauty of sex. The story of the rape of Dinah in Genesis tells of the explosive and destructive nature of the sexual instinct when it goes wrong. The Bible tells about life as it is! That one act of rape led to untold misery. All down the history of the human race, the misuse of sex has caused misery and distress. Wars have begun and continued because of it. Today, families are broken, people's lives are torn apart, with violence erupting, even murder committed, because of sexual infidelities of one kind or another.

The sex instinct is a beautiful instinct, as we have seen the Scriptures tell us. It is the basis not only of procreation, but of so much which is good in us: our friendships, our affectivity. Psychologists would echo these words of the Catechism:

2332 *Sexuality* affects all aspects of the human person in the unity of his body and soul. It especially concerns

21

affectivity, the capacity to love and to procreate, and in a more general way the aptitude for forming bonds of communion with others.

The sexual drive in all of us can be used positively, whether we are married or single, priest or lay person. On the other hand, it is also a time-bomb ticking inside each one of us, which can explode destructively unless controlled:

> Love is strong as death, passion fierce as the grave;
> Its flashes are flashes of fire, a raging flame.
> Many waters cannot quench love, neither can floods drown it.
>
> Song of Solomon 8:6-7

How, then, do we tame this beautiful but wild and potentially dangerous animal pent up inside each one of us? That is precisely what this book is about.

2

The desire of the heart

Q. What is the basis of Catholic sexual ethics?

A.   To find the basics of Catholic sexual ethics, we must go much further back than sex itself, to find the basics of all morality. Whatever we do, we do because we want something, for ourselves or for someone else. We try to fulfil our desires as human beings. Catholic morals are based, first and foremost, not on rules and regulations, but upon a human desire for God, upon which all other desires and needs find their rationale. As the *Catechism of the Catholic Church* states:

> 27   The desire for God is written in the human heart, because man is created by God and for God; and God never ceases to draw man to himself. Only in God will he find the truth and happiness he never stops searching for.

The Catechism then goes on to quote the famous St Augustine of Hippo.

> 30   You are great, O Lord, and greatly to be praised: great is your power and your wisdom is without measure.

And man, so small a part of your creation, wants to praise you: this man, though clothed with mortality and bearing the evidence of sin and the proof that you withstand the proud. Despite everything, man, though but a small a part of your creation, wants to praise you. You yourself encourage him to delight in your praise, for you have made us for yourself, and our heart is restless until it rests in you.

Augustine was a great saint and theological genius. But he was not always interested in Catholic theology. Indeed, in his wild and impetuous youth, he had a mistress, who gave him a son, Adeodatus. So Augustine knew very well what it meant to desire things other than God. But he was restless in his mind, seeking to satisfy his religious instincts with a heretical sect called the Mandaeans. His clever mind soon spotted the pitfalls in this 'new age' kind of religion. But he continued to be unhappy, until he was walking in a garden and picked up the Scriptures, turning the page at random, finding a text from St Paul which changed his life:

The night is far gone, the day is near. Let us then lay aside the works of darkness and put on the armour of light; let us live honourably as in the day, not in revelling and drunkenness, not in debauchery and licentiousness, not in quarrelling and jealousy. Instead, put on the Lord Jesus Christ, and make no provision for the flesh, to gratify its desires.

Romans 13:12-14

Augustine then realised that he had to make a radical turnaround. He became a great Catholic bishop and writer, but he did continue to care for and provide for his illegitimate son. From living for his flesh, just to satisfy the desires of his body, he had to follow God. This God, he now understood, had created him, Augustine, for himself, and God was his only source of happiness.

Q. But that seems quite absurd. Surely many people find happiness in all kinds of ordinary things; in a job, in their marriage, in sport, in music. Why is God our only source of final happiness?

A. God does want us to be happy in the ordinary things of life. After all, he has given us a world to live in, one in which he wants us to be happy. But we are created with an immortal soul, a mind which yearns for the infinite. We are not just a body with its needs to be fulfilled. This immortal soul will always make us dissatisfied with anything less than loving and knowing the God who made us for that purpose, and for nothing less.

A famous wealthy industrialist was asked why he continued to work sixteen hours a day, when he already had enough money to last the rest of his life. 'I make more money, in order to buy more businesses.' 'But why buy more businesses?' asked the interviewer. 'I buy more businesses in order to make more money to buy more businesses. It is a kind of obsession.'

That wealthy man indicates that the mind is not satisfied with anything less than the infinite. In his case, it led him to try to make an infinite amount of money! Desire for material possessions will always lead to dissatisfaction, because the nature of the human person is to desire God, who created us, and who is the only infinite source of love.

Any created happiness will leave something for us to desire more. Our final happiness, which St Thomas Aquinas calls in Latin *beatitudo,* blessedness, can only be in God:

> It is impossible for the happiness of the human being to be fully happy (*beatitudo*) in any created good. For *beatitudo* is a perfect good, which totally satisfies the appetite; for otherwise it is not the ultimate end, if there remains something else to be desired. For the object of the will, which is the human appetite, is the universal good; just as the object of the intellect is the universal

truth. From this it is obvious that nothing can quieten the human will, except the universal good. This is not found in any created object, but only in God: because every creature has only participated goodness. Therefore only God can fulfil the desire of the human will; as it says in the Psalms [102:5] *Who fulfils your desire with good things.*

Summa Theologiae, 1-2, q.2, a.8

And we will eventually have to leave all our possessions to go to meet the God who made us, and who is our only final happiness. This is what the wealthy man in the Gospel parable told by Jesus found out too late:

And Jesus said to them, 'Take care! Be on your guard against all kinds of greed; for one's life does not consist in the abundance of possessions.'

Then he told them a parable: 'The land of a rich man produced abundantly. And he thought to himself, "What should I do, for I have no place to store my crops?" Then he said, "I will do this: I will pull down my barns and build larger ones, and there I will store all my grain and my goods. And I will say to my soul: 'Soul, you have ample goods laid up for many years; relax, eat, drink, be merry.'"

But God said to him, 'You fool! This very night your life is being demanded of you. And the things you have prepared, whose will they be?' So it is with those who store up treasures for themselves but are not rich toward God.'

Luke 12:15-21

Q. But most people have ordinary needs, supplied day by day, for food, job satisfaction, human love. Surely, all this business of a desire for God is way above most people's expectations or needs?

A. Modern life is capitalist and consumer led. It tries to make us stifle this need for the infinite; and, we must admit, is making a very good job of it! But the yearning for drugs among young people, the suicide rate alarmingly increasing, these are indications of dissatisfaction. One young man, who committed suicide in prison, said simply that he had experienced everything life had to offer and there was nothing else; so why not 'top himself'? All this is only a sign that there is a deeper yearning in the human heart for spiritual satisfaction, for something to give a silver lining to the cloud of most people's dull lives.

We work very hard to make sure that people do not suffer handicap and are able to fulfil their full human potential. We teach blind people Braille in order that their sight problem does not deny them the human skill to be able to read and write. A person who does not develop a relationship with God is simply blind, spiritually blind. See John's Gospel chapter 9, the cure of the blind man by Jesus. We need his healing first and foremost to see the need for God.

Q. But how can the desire for God compete with the great sensations of life: sex, a winning football team, winning the Lottery?

A. Scripture tells us that the joys of seeing God in heaven, our eternal destiny ordained by God, are much greater than any earthly joy: 'But, as it is written, "What no eye has seen, nor ear heard, nor the human heart conceived, what God has prepared for those who love him"' – these things God has revealed to us through the Spirit; for the Spirit searches everything, even the depths of God (1 Cor 2:9-10).

There are people who have had a special experience of God. They are sometimes called visionaries or mystics. They tell us that any true experience of God is way above any other experience we might have in life, even above sex! The Bible puts it that a person who experiences God in a special way 'sees the glory of God' (Jn 11:40).

One great experience of the glory of God was when three disciples of Jesus went up a mountain in Galilee, and had a vision of who Jesus really was. Up to then, they had seen very much a human being, even if this human being was very special, performing miracles of healing, exorcisms, and speaking stunning words about the coming Kingdom of God. But, then, on the holy mountain, they saw just a glimpse of the real Jesus, in his glory, as the only begotten Son of God:

> Six days later, Jesus took with him Peter and James and his brother John and led them up a high mountain, by themselves. And he was transfigured before them, and his face shone like the sun, and his clothes became dazzling white. Suddenly there appeared to them Moses and Elijah, talking with him. Then Peter said to Jesus, 'Lord, it is good for us to be here; if you wish, I will make three dwellings here, one for you, one for Moses, and one for Elijah.' While he was still speaking, suddenly a bright cloud overshadowed them, and from the cloud a voice said, 'This is my Son, the Beloved; with him I am well pleased; listen to him!' When the disciples heard this, they fell to the ground and were overcome by fear. But Jesus came and touched them, saying, 'Get up and do not be afraid.' And when they looked up, they saw no one except Jesus himself alone.
>
> Matthew 17:1-8

For Peter, James and John, this wonderful experience of seeing the transfigured Jesus was a fleeting moment. Straight after they all descended that mountain, Jesus led them on the long walk from Galilee to Jerusalem, where he was to be put to a shameful and excruciating death on the cross.

Mystical experiences for most of us are rare events; although most people who pray regularly experience something of the joys of life with God which will only take place fully after death. But the experience of millions of Christians down the centuries is that living with Christ the Christian life, and knowing that the future is infinitely better, makes all the ups and downs worth while. And it transforms an ordinary life on earth to being special, because that life is seen *sub specie aeternitatae* (under the aspect of eternity). No one understood this better than St Paul, the great apostle of the early days of the Church:

> Who will separate us from the love of Christ? Will hardship, or distress, or persecution, or famine, or nakedness, or peril, or sword? As it is written, 'For your sake we are being killed all day long; we are accounted as sheep to be slaughtered.' No, in all these things we are more than conquerors through him who loved us. For I am convinced that neither death, nor life, nor angels, nor rulers, nor things present, nor things to come, nor powers, nor height, nor depth, nor anything else in all creation, will be able to separate us from the love of God in Christ Jesus our Lord.
>
> Romans 8:35-39

St Paul would say, with this in mind, who would want anything else? In fact, you might even say that the Christian is the most selfish person on earth, the most activated by self-interest. If we were offered a million pounds in the bank to finish the London Marathon, most of us would at least have a go. It might even be worth the risk of a heart attack for one not too athletically minded! Such would not be heroics, but sheer self-interest, a million-pound cheque after we have crossed the finishing line. But as Paul says, we do not run the race of this life for 'a perishable wreath' (Cor 9:25). We are due to collect much more than a million pounds after we die. We have the prize awaiting us of the calling of Christ Jesus, the crown of eternal life, of joy with God and all the saints which we cannot imagine here on earth. Even self-interest would say, is it not worth the trade?

Jesus said as much, in his parable of the treasure and of the pearl:

> The Kingdom of Heaven is like treasure hidden in a field, which someone found and hid; then in his joy he goes and sells all that he has and buys that field.
>
> Again, the Kingdom of Heaven is like a merchant in search of fine pearls; on finding one pearl of great value, he went and sold all that he had and bought it.
>
> Matthew 13:44-46

God has given us something to want, himself the supreme object of our human desire. But, in the parables above, Jesus tells us that in order to possess this treasure hidden in the field of this world and all its wants, this pearl of great price suddenly discovered among all the cheap trash, we have to sell everything we have in order to buy it.

What does that mean?

3

How we get it

Q. How, then, do we attain to this God who is our final desire and destiny?

A. By doing what is good, and not doing what is evil. The *Catechism of the Catholic Church* sums up our programme of action as human beings:

> 1702 The divine image is present in every man. It shines forth in the communion of persons, in the likeness of the union of the divine persons among themselves (cf chapter 2).

> 1703 Endowed with 'a spiritual and immortal' soul, the human person is 'the only creature on earth that God has willed for its own sake'. From his conception, he is destined for eternal beatitude.

> 1704 The human person participates in the light and power of the divine Spirit. By his reason, he is capable of understanding the order of things established by the Creator. By free will, he is capable of directing himself toward his true good. He finds his perfection 'in seeking and loving what is true and good'.

1705 By virtue of his soul and his spiritual powers of intellect and will, man is endowed with freedom, an 'outstanding manifestation of the divine image'.

1706 By his reason, man recognises the voice of God which urges him 'to do what is good and avoid what is evil'. Everyone is obliged to follow this law, which makes itself heard in conscience and is fulfilled in the love of God and of neighbour. Living a moral life bears witness to the dignity of the person.

You see the argument.

- We are all made in God's image.
- This gives us a supreme dignity and a supreme vocation.
- We are destined for eternal blessedness because of that immortal soul which we possess, directly created by God.
- We attain that blessedness by acting just as we are, that is, by directing ourselves to what is truly good.
- Being created with an immortal soul, we are free to choose the good, not like lower animals which act by instinct.
- We know what that good is through our reason.
- We are obliged to follow what we know is right.

When we buy a washing machine, we find that it functions best if we use it as a washing machine, and not as a television. If we want to find out how to work the washing machine, we look to the instructions of the maker.

So with ourselves and our moral conduct: the Catechism is here telling us that, if we wish to find happiness, that final happiness which is our vocation as human beings for all eternity, we must act according our Maker's instructions, God himself. We must discover first what is right, and then act according to it. And the Church teaches us that our reason should know what is right, because that is what we are made for, for what is good. The Maker's instructions are written in ourselves as humans, in our human nature.

Q. Why, then, do we do what is not right, what is not according to our reason?

A. That is at least partly because of what we call Original Sin, sin from the beginning (Latin *ab origine).* From the very beginning, human beings disobeyed God, and we are suffering the consequences. As the Catechism says:

> 390 The account of the fall in Genesis 3 uses figurative language, but affirms a primeval event, a deed that took place *at the beginning of the history of man.* Revelation gives us the certainty of faith that the whole of human history is marked by the original fault freely committed by our first parents.

This Fall causes a problem regarding our human nature:

> 1707 'Man, enticed by the Evil One, abused his freedom at the very beginning of history.' He succumbed to temptation and did what was evil. He still desires the good, but his nature bears the wound of original sin. He is now inclined to evil and subject to error:
>
>> Man is divided in himself. As a result, the whole life of men, both individual and social, shows itself to be a struggle, and a dramatic one, between good and evil, between light and darkness. (Vatican II, *Gaudium et Spes,* Constitution on the Church in the Modern World, No. 13.)

So, the Church tells us, we can know what is right, but our reason has been harmed by Original Sin so that we are inclined to do what is wrong; just like a car with defective steering. This affects us both as individuals and as a human community, especially, as we shall see soon, regarding sexual ethics. Sin obscures our knowledge of what is right, and inclines us to act towards the evil rather than towards the good. St Paul, that great missionary, could still see the problem after many years of Christian service:

> So I find it to be a law that when I want to do what is good, evil lies close at hand. For I delight in the law of God in my inmost self, but I see in my members another law at war with the law of my mind, making me captive to the law of sin that dwells in my members. Wretched man that I am! Who will rescue me from this body of death?
>
> Romans 7:21-24

Q. What, then, is the solution to this?

A. It is a continuous struggle, as Paul says. But it is one that we can win, with God's help. God has provided a plan of salvation, to correct this fault and bring us back into friendship. First, four thousand years ago, he called a people led by the patriarch Abraham (see Gen 12). Then, after three generations, he brought them miraculously out of Egypt, from slavery, to conquer the Promised Land, now called Israel. On their journey, he gave them the Ten Commandments, which were to be their basic moral code, both as individuals and as a community, his very own people.

Q. But are not these Ten Commandments a little outmoded?

A. Not at all. They express what we considered at the beginning of this chapter, the law of our being, written in our human nature, i.e. the Natural Law. They are revelation, in Scripture, the Word of God. But they find their basis also in that law of right and wrong written in our hearts:

1954 Man participates in the wisdom and goodness of the Creator who gives him mastery over his acts and the ability to govern himself with a view to the true and the good. The natural law expresses the original moral sense which enables man to discern by reason the good and the evil, the truth and the lie:

> The natural law is written and engraved in the soul of each and every man, because it is human reason ordaining him to do good and forbidding him to sin… But this command of human reason would not have the force of law if it were not the voice and interpreter of a higher reason to which our spirit and our freedom must be submitted.
>
> Pope Leo XIII

1955 The 'divine and natural' law shows man the way to follow so as to practise the good and attain his end. The natural law states the first and essential precepts which govern the moral life. It hinges upon the desire for God and submission to him, who is the source and judge of all that is good, as well as upon the sense that the other is one's equal. Its principal precepts are expressed in the Decalogue. This law is called 'natural', not in reference to the nature of irrational beings, but because reason which decrees it properly belongs to human nature.

We must make sure that we do not confuse the Church's teaching about the Natural Law with laws of nature uncovered by natural science; although the laws of human biology are of course related to the natural moral law. The Catechism makes this distinction clear. The Natural Law in the moral sense is discovered – when our moral reason is working correctly – by our reflection as human beings upon our nature as made in God's image and likeness, and what follows from that rational human nature in terms of action. And also, as the Catechism says, these precepts of the Natural Law are expressed in the Decalogue, that is, in the Ten Commandments.

Q. What is the most important of all the Commandments?

A. Jesus gave the answer to this question while on earth. He was asked by a theologian of that time: 'Teacher, which commandment in the law is the greatest?' Jesus said to him, 'You shall love the Lord your God with all your heart, and with all your soul, and with all your mind. This is the greatest and first commandment' (Mt 22:36-8).

What Jesus says follows logically from what we have seen so far. If we are made for God, and our only final happiness lies in our Creator, then to love God himself is the greatest commandment. Nothing can compare with it, even loving our neighbour, which is the second commandment. The first and greatest commandment is the foundation of all other commandments, written in Scripture, confirmed by Jesus, but written in our hearts as created beings made in God's image and likeness. It is the first and greatest precept of the Natural Law, as well as the first commandment in Scripture.

God is to be loved in himself, and for no other reason. Even committed Christians today have tended to lose this sense of the transcendence of God, worshipped, loved and adored in himself and for himself. In trying to make religion socially relevant, here is the danger in this secular world of always trying to justify what we do in terms of humanist ethics. We are always on a loser if we try to do this.

Jesus points in another direction, upwards. He directs us daily to develop a relationship to God our heavenly Father in prayer, and to join in public worship of God. For this reason, the Catholic Church makes the weekly attendance at Mass an obligation, precisely to fulfil this obligation to love God, the first and greatest commandment.

36

St Paul roots the sexual depravity of the Roman Empire in which he was living to disobedience to the first commandment. Paul accuses the pagans of his day:

> For though they knew God, they did not honour him as God or give thanks to him, but they became futile in their thinking, and their senseless minds were darkened. Claiming to be wise, they became fools; and they exchanged the glory of the immortal God for images resembling a mortal human being or birds or four-footed animals or reptiles. Therefore God gave them up in the lusts of their hearts to impurity, to the degrading of their bodies among themselves, because they exchanged the truth about God for a lie and worshiped and served the creature rather than the Creator, who is blessed forever! Amen
>
> Romans 1:21-25

Paul sounds a bit hard on the Gentiles here. But he is making just the points we have tried to emphasise in this chapter. All people, including those who have not any specific revelation such as the Jews had through Scripture, have the Natural Law written in their hearts. The first commandment of that Law is to worship God alone. If the first commandment is disobeyed, then we human beings will soon treat with contempt God's creatures like ourselves. We will not respect either our bodies or theirs; and impurity and immorality will be the result, as it was in the empire of Paul's day, and in ours!

Q. Have not Christians sometimes forgotten their fellow human beings in worshipping God alone, and for himself?

A. This should never happen; although unfortunately it sometimes does, because we Christians are not perfect! The opposite should be the case, that worshipping God as our Creator should lead to respecting our fellow humans. This is why we must always balance the second commandment given by Jesus with the first: 'And a second is like it: "You shall love your neighbour as yourself"' (Mt 22:39).

As a very early Christian warned his fellow Christians, 'Those who say, "I love God," and hate their brothers or sisters, are liars; for those who do not love a brother or sister whom they have seen, cannot love God whom they have not seen. The commandment we have from him [Jesus] is this: "those who love God must love their brothers and sisters also"' (1 Jn 4:20-21).

The second commandment, and the second precept of the Natural Law, then, is to love our neighbour as ourselves. The word 'neighbour' here means 'those near to us' that is, everybody with whom we come into contact. So we can count the whole human race as our neighbour! Particularly after the coming of Christ, the Son of God, who took our human nature, the whole of the human race are brothers and sisters. Jesus took our human nature, that is everyone's human nature. That is why racial hatred is so entirely incompatible with Christian ethics. We love our neighbour as ourself because each human being is equally made in the image and likeness of God, as we are.

This makes sense of the Ten Commandments. Traditional Christianity divided the Ten Commandments up into two Tablets, two stones on which Moses received the written Words of God.

The first table
('"You shall love the Lord your God with all your heart, and with all your soul, and with all your mind." This is the greatest and first Commandment.')

1. I AM THE LORD YOUR GOD; YOU SHALL NOT HAVE STRANGE GODS BEFORE ME. Our first duty is to worship God, and nothing else.

2. YOU SHALL NOT TAKE THE NAME OF THE LORD YOUR GOD IN VAIN. God is our creator. We must not treat him with disrespect.

3. REMEMBER TO KEEP HOLY THE LORD'S DAY. We must rest from our work, and worship God one day out of seven.

The second table

('And a second is like it: "You shall love your neighbour as yourself."')

4. HONOUR YOUR FATHER AND YOUR MOTHER. We treat our parents with great love and respect, as those who gave us life and nourishment.

5. YOU SHALL NOT KILL. We view other human beings like ourselves, made in God's image and likeness. We cannot kill innocent life.

6. **YOU SHALL NOT COMMIT ADULTERY. The sin of infidelity in marriage offends against the law of Genesis, that the two, man and woman, become one flesh. Adultery breaks this divinely commanded union.**

7. YOU SHALL NOT STEAL. We respect what people have legitimately acquired as their own, because we respect them.

8. YOU SHALL NOT BEAR FALSE WITNESS AGAINST YOUR NEIGHBOUR. It is against the law of God written in our nature to harm another human being because of our lies.

9. **YOU SHALL NOT COVET YOUR NEIGHBOUR'S WIFE. As Jesus said, 'You have heard that it was said, "You shall not commit adultery." But I say to you that everyone who looks at a woman with lust has already committed adultery with her in his heart' (Mt 5:27-8).**

10. YOU SHALL NOT COVET YOUR NEIGHBOUR'S GOODS.
    Envy is a dangerous emotion. We should delight in the
    good of another's success, not want to grasp it for
    ourselves. This is to share in God's own generosity.

We see that two commandments are related specially to
sexuality, the sixth and ninth commandments. We shall be
focusing on those two commandments, again rooted in the
Natural Law, in the rest of this book. But we will fail to
understand the Church's teaching on sexuality unless we
have the whole picture as to the basis of the Christian life
as expounded by the teaching authority of the Catholic
Church. That is why we have looked at the wider basis of
morality in this present chapter.

4

Jesus and sex

Q. I wondered when we were getting round to Jesus. We have said little about him and his teaching so far. I thought that the Catholic Church claimed to base its teaching on Jesus?

A. We have mentioned him from time to time! However, it has been quite deliberate, to leave a full discussion on his teaching until now. We have emphasised that Catholic moral teaching is founded on the Natural Law, written in our hearts with our human nature. This was, as we have seen, known long before the coming of Jesus. It is also important to emphasise that Catholic moral teaching claims to be not just for Christians, or even for those who believe in the One God – Jews, Moslems and Christians. Because it is based upon the Natural Law, the basic ethics of the Church applies to all faiths, to all people.

Also, Jesus was himself a Jew, born of a Jewish mother, Mary. He made it clear that he accepted the Jewish Law, given from the time of Moses onwards. He said explicitly: 'Do not think that I have come to abolish the law or the prophets; I have come not to abolish but to fulfil' (Mt 5:17). Scholars today are emphasising more and more the Jewishness of Jesus. Jesus also reaffirmed the Ten

Commandments, in an encounter with a rich young ruler who was seeking to become his disciple:

> As Jesus was setting out on a journey, a man ran up and knelt before him, and asked him, 'Good Teacher, what must I do to inherit eternal life?' Jesus said to him, 'Why do you call me good? No one is good but God alone. You know the commandments: "You shall not murder; You shall not commit adultery; You shall not steal; You shall not bear false witness; You shall not defraud; Honour your father and mother."' He said to him, 'Teacher, I have kept all these since my youth.'
>
> Mark 10:17-20

Clearly, Jesus expected his hearers to know and to obey the Commandments, if they wanted 'life'; that is true life with God, following his Way. Jesus did not see himself as coming in to bring a totally new law, but to reinforce the old law, and impose his own authoritative interpretation as the New Moses, the Son of God become Man. So the first thing we have to do to follow Jesus is to obey the Ten Commandments!

Q. What, then, was new about the teaching of Jesus?

A. First, Jesus claimed to bring what he saw as a higher standard of obedience to God than did some of the theologians who were his contemporaries. He said, provocatively:

> For I tell you, unless your righteousness exceeds that of the scribes and Pharisees, you will never enter the Kingdom of Heaven. You have heard that it was said to those of ancient times, 'You shall not murder'; and 'whoever murders shall be liable to judgement.' But I say to you that if you are angry with a brother or sister, you will be liable to judgement; and if you insult a brother or sister, you will be liable to the council; and if

you say, 'You fool,' you will be liable to the hell of fire. So when you are offering your gift at the altar, if you remember that your brother or sister has something against you, leave your gift there before the altar and go; first be reconciled to your brother or sister, and then come and offer your gift.

Matthew 5:20-24

It is only too easy to use the Gospels to become anti-Semitic. That is quite wrong. Jesus claimed to be teaching a higher kind of righteousness than the theologians of his day, the two schools of the Sadducees and the Pharisees. But that was an internal dispute within Judaism of that time. Jesus was as much a Jew as the scribes and Pharisees with whom he disputed. In a similar way, various schools of thought dispute within the Catholic Church.

But Jesus did consider that his interpretation was right, and that it was better than other views at his time. It was better because it emphasised the heart. The Hebrew word means much more than the pump which circulates blood around the body: it means the seat of all the emotions, and the human will which motivates us whatever we do. So Jesus emphasised that not only the external act (e.g. murder) was wrong. Anger and hatred were also wrong. This was not entirely new. The ninth and tenth commandments, 'You shall not covet' are both commandments relating not to actions but to interior motivations. But the emphasis of Jesus was new here, and the boldness with which he put his teaching across.

Just as with murder, Jesus says that the act of adultery itself is not the only sin. Just as anger can be a sin of the heart, so a man can sin in his heart by lust:

You have heard that it was said, 'You shall not commit adultery.' But I say to you that everyone who looks at a woman with lust has already committed adultery with her in his heart. If your right eye causes you to sin, tear it out and throw it away; it is better for you to lose one of your members than for your whole body to be thrown into hell. And if your right hand causes you to sin, cut it off and throw it away; it is better for you to lose one of your members than for your whole body to go into hell.

Matthew 5:27-30

No one could accuse Jesus of being lax where sexual morality is concerned! Some have accused St Augustine of bringing a rigid puritan attitude to sexuality into Christianity. But, if a person wishes to attack the Christian view of sex, you must begin right with Jesus. In the above quotation, he is saying that a lustful thought is itself adultery in the heart. (Incidentally, to avoid scruples at this point, later we will make the clear distinction between temptation in the mind to lust, and consent in the mind to impurity. The latter is a sin, the former is not. The sin of lust implies an act of the will consenting, whereas the temptation does not in itself imply consent of the will.)

This is tough talking on sexuality. Jesus goes even further in that same text. He says that it is better to remove an offending member of the body than to go into hell with the heart full of lust. The early Church Father Origen imprudently castrated himself on the basis of the above text of Jesus. Better to go to heaven without it, than to hell with it! The Church condemned Origen for this foolish action. The Catholic Church does not allow dismemberment except for serious medical reasons, such as a cancerous breast being removed to save the whole body.

Jesus, of course, was speaking metaphorically! But he was not speaking metaphorically concerning the need to govern our thoughts, and the danger if we do not. What was new and radical was his teaching about all foods being ritually clean. Most likely, during his lifetime, Jesus expected his disciples to obey the ritual laws of Judaism. These would cleanse ritually; but not the heart. That had to be cleansed from within, by repentance, change of heart.

Then he called the crowd again and said to them, 'Listen to me, all of you, and understand: there is nothing outside a person that by going in can defile, but the things that come out are what defile.' When he had left the crowd and entered the house, his disciples asked him about the parable. He said to them, 'Then do you also fail to understand? Do you not see that whatever goes into a person from outside cannot defile, since it enters, not the heart but the stomach, and goes out into the sewer?' (Thus he declared all foods clean.) And he said, 'It is what comes out of a person that defiles. For it is from within, from the human heart, that evil intentions come: fornication, theft, murder, adultery, avarice, wickedness, deceit, licentiousness, envy, slander, pride, folly. All these evil things come from within, and they defile a person.'

Mark 7:14-23

Q. Jesus was against divorce too, was he not?

A. Most certainly. His views would have been considered quite extreme. He was asked a question relating to a dispute between the rabbis. The strict view was that a man could divorce his wife only for her infidelity. The lenient view was that he could divorce her for burning the toast. What was his view? Jesus shocked all his hearers:

Some Pharisees came to Jesus, and to test him they asked, 'Is it lawful for a man to divorce his wife for any cause?' He answered, 'Have you not read that the one who made them at the beginning "made them male and female," and said, "For this reason a man shall leave his father and mother and be joined to his wife, and the two shall become one flesh?" So they are no longer two, but one flesh. Therefore what God has joined together, let no one separate.' They said to him, 'Why then did Moses command us to give a certificate of dismissal

45

and to divorce her?' He said to them, 'It was because you were so hard-hearted that Moses allowed you to divorce your wives, but from the beginning it was not so. And I say to you, whoever divorces his wife, except for unchastity, and marries another commits adultery.'

Matthew 19:3-9

We will have to return to this text later for a more detailed interpretation, when we look more closely at the whole question of divorce, remarriage, and marriage annulment. What is clear even at first glance, however, is that Jesus is quite radical here. He goes back to Genesis, a text we viewed in the first chapter of this book. Jesus says that from the beginning it was God's purpose that man and woman should be united in sexual union, and that that union should never be broken in their lifetime. The two should become one flesh, and stay one flesh.

We will be taking a particular look at the phrase in 19:9 'except for unchastity' later on. Sufficient it is to say here that it does not take away the force of the judgement of Jesus here. For him, there is no divorce whatsoever. A divorcee who remarries simply commits adultery, in his view.

Q. Jesus also favoured a celibate life, did he not?

A. That depends what you mean by 'favoured. He himself was unmarried. His public ministry only lasted three years, after which he was crucified. He also led the life of an itinerant preacher and miracle worker, which would have been most difficult for a wife to follow. But there seems to have been a deeper reason. Jesus said For in the resurrection they neither marry nor are given in marriage, but are like angels in heaven' (Mt 22:30). Since he was preaching the Kingdom of Heaven, it would seem natural to him to anticipate this Kingdom by himself remaining unmarried.

This would seem to be the simplest explanation of the

following text. His disciples, yet once more shocked by what their Rabbi said about divorce, made the most obvious reactive reply:

> His disciples said to him, 'If such is the case of a man with his wife, it is better not to marry.' But he said to them, 'Not everyone can accept this teaching, but only those to whom it is given. For there are eunuchs who have been so from birth, and there are eunuchs who have been made eunuchs by others, and there are eunuchs who have made themselves eunuchs for the sake of the Kingdom of Heaven. Let anyone accept this who can.'
>
> Matthew 19:10-12

The reaction of his disciples to Jesus' words about divorce is quite natural. It is better not to marry than to tie yourself up with a woman for life without any escape clause! But Jesus' reply here is still even more surprising. The plain meaning of the text is that Jesus is encouraging voluntary celibacy for the Kingdom of Heaven, but only for those who can accept it, i.e. for those who have a vocation for celibacy. His own celibacy was most certainly for the 'Kingdom of Heaven'. Jesus here is giving a pattern for the future vocation of Christians, which again we will have to discuss more fully later.

Q. With all this strict teaching about sex, however did Jesus acquire any followers?

A. A fair question! We will see in the next chapter that the key is the gift of the Holy Spirit, given to the apostles at the day of Pentecost after his resurrection and so to all the disciples of Jesus. The Holy Spirit makes possible a new way of obedience to God, with the power of God within. This would fulfil the prophecy of Jeremiah about a new covenant, a new spirit, so that people would know God and willingly follow his Way (Jer 31:31). This interior spirit would make Jesus' yoke easy and his burden light.

The second factor was Jesus' forgiveness of sinners, especially of those who had committed sexual sins. Jesus was accused of eating with sinners. And above all, we have the wonderful story of the forgiveness of the woman who had been caught committing adultery:

> Jesus bent down and wrote with his finger on the ground. When they kept on questioning him, he straightened up and said to them, 'Let anyone among you who is without sin be the first to throw a stone at her.' And once again he bent down and wrote on the ground. When they heard it, they went away, one by one, beginning with the elders; and Jesus was left alone with the woman standing before him. Jesus straightened up and said to her, 'Woman, where are they? Has no one condemned you?' She said, 'No one, sir.' And Jesus said, 'Neither do I condemn you. Go your way, and from now on do not sin again.'
>
> John 8:6-11

There is the whole tradition of the Church's confessional practice begun with Jesus. It is not an 'easy touch'. Jesus commands her not to sin again. But that woman has the knowledge that she can make another start to follow the right way. She is motivated to begin the life of the Beatitudes, the summary of the morality of Jesus.

In the Beatitudes, Jesus himself tells us where true happiness lies on this earth. And it is the opposite to what the world- tells us constitutes happiness:

> When Jesus saw the crowds, he went up the mountain; and after he sat down, his disciples came to him. Then he began to speak, and taught them, saying:
> 'Blessed are the poor in spirit, for theirs is the Kingdom of Heaven.
> Blessed are those who mourn, for they will be comforted.

Blessed are the meek, for they will inherit the earth.

Blessed are those who hunger and thirst for righteousness, for they will be filled.

Blessed are the merciful, for they will receive mercy.

Blessed are the pure in heart, for they will see God.

Blessed are the peacemakers, for they will be called children of God.

Blessed are those who are persecuted for righteousness' sake, for theirs is the Kingdom of Heaven.

Blessed are you when people revile you and persecute you and utter all kinds of evil against you falsely on my account. Rejoice and be glad, for your reward is great in heaven, for in the same way they persecuted the prophets who were before you.

You are the salt of the earth; but if salt has lost its taste, how can its saltiness be restored? It is no longer good for anything, but is thrown out and trampled under foot.

You are the light of the world. A city built on a hill cannot be hid. No one after lighting a lamp puts it under the bushel basket, but on the lamp-stand, and it gives light to all in the house. In the same way, let your light shine before others, so that they may see your good works and give glory to your Father in heaven.'

Matthew 5:1-16

How can anyone live such a life? By their own strength, that is impossible. But with the Spirit, all things are possible.

5

St Paul and sex

Q. What is so special about St Paul?

A. St Paul was not only the first Christian missionary to the Gentiles. In his letters to the various churches he founded all over the Roman Empire, Paul laid the foundations of Christian theology for all time. He never knew Jesus during his life on earth. Paul was converted from persecuting Christians to be their strongest advocate after witnessing the stoning to death of the first Christian martyr, St Stephen.

We all know the dramatic story of Paul's conversion on the Damascus Road, when he was travelling to Damascus with letters from the authorities in Jerusalem to arrest members of the new Christian sect there. We all know how Paul was dazzled by a shining light, and fell to the ground from his mount. How he heard a voice saying 'Saul, Saul, why do you persecute me? (Acts 9:4). (Saul was his other name.) Paul replied, 'Who are you, Lord?' As a good Jewish theologian, an up and coming rabbi, Paul knew well that visions in the Old Testament were often accompanied by light or fire, like the burning bush which Moses saw on the mountain (Ex 3:2).

Who, then, was this Lord, manifesting himself to Paul? The divine voiced replied, 'I am Jesus, whom you are persecuting' (Acts 9:5). Paul was baptised a Christian when he eventually arrived at Damascus, and, after a period of preparation and reflection (*see* Gal 1:15–2:1) began his phenomenally successful mission.

It did not bother Paul that he did not know Jesus during Jesus' earthly life. For Paul, what really mattered was believing that Jesus was truly the exalted Lord, risen from the dead, and receiving his Spirit in baptism. Paul saw Jesus as Lord, the God come to save us. Perhaps the clearest expression of his creed is in the hymn he sent to the Christians at Philippi, to encourage them to maintain their faith and perseverance under persecution:

> Let the same mind be in you that was in Christ Jesus, who, though he was in the form of God, did not regard equality with God as something to be exploited, but emptied himself, taking the form of a slave, being born in human likeness. And being found in human form, he humbled himself and became obedient to the point of death – even death on a cross. Therefor God also highly exalted him and gave him the name that is above every name, so that at the name of Jesus every knee would bend, in heaven and on earth and under the earth, and every tongue should confess that Jesus Christ is Lord, to the glory of God the Father.
>
> Phil 2:5-11

It seems clear that Paul is here proclaiming the divinity of Christ. It would be blasphemy to 'bend the knee' at anyone but God (*see* Is 45:23). For Paul, the word for God (in Greek *ho theos*) always refers to God the Father. But the title he uses for Jesus, Lord (in Greek *ho kurios*), is in fact the other name for God in the Old Testament. It was the special name for the God who revealed himself to Moses on that holy mountain as I AM WHO I AM (Ex 3:14).

We cannot understand anything about St Paul, especially his sexual ethics, until we understand this: that for him,

Jesus is now the Lord of all creation, and that we are all summoned to become members of his body, the Church. In ethics, then, as in everything else, for Paul, Jesus must have the last word!

Q. But did not Paul say that the Law had come to an end with Christ?

A. Not regarding the Ten Commandments. The 'Law' here for Paul meant the ceremonial precepts of the law, like the ritual of circumcision, which was replaced by baptism. It also meant that, for Paul, the Law was unable to save us from our sins. That could only be given freely by Christ through his grace (*see* Gal 3).

But Paul was quite clear that as Christians we had to continue to obey the Ten Commandments:

> Owe no one anything, except to love one another; for the one who loves another has fulfilled the law. The commandments, 'You shall not commit adultery; You shall not murder; You shall not steal; You shall not covet'; and any other commandment, are summed up in this word, 'Love your neighbour as yourself.' Love does no wrong to a neighbour; therefore, love is the fulfilling of the law.
>
> Romans 13:8-10

Paul was also clear that these commandments were written in the heart of everyone, whether Jew or Gentile. He believed in the Natural Law in the sense we have described earlier. For Paul, Gentiles could obey the Ten Commandments even if they had never seen those commandments written in the Bible, because they were written in their nature:

> For it is not the hearers of the law who are righteous in God's sight, but the doers of the law who will be

justified. When Gentiles, who do not possess the law, do instinctively what the law requires, these, though not having the law, are a law to themselves. They show that what the law requires is written on their hearts, to which their own conscience also bears witness; and their conflicting thoughts will accuse or perhaps excuse them.

Romans 2:13-15

Paul, then, taught the same springs of morality as did Jesus: the Natural Law as expressed definitively in the Ten Commandments.

Q. But was not Paul pessimistic about sex?

A. Not at all. Rather, he had a very exalted view of the sexual act, which came from his Jewish roots. The sexual act was two human beings becoming one flesh, i.e. one person, as in the Genesis text we saw in the first chapter.

This becomes clear when we look at the way in which Paul responds to a case of incest as reported to him from Corinth, which was the sex capital of the Roman Empire. Corinth was settled by retired Roman soldiers, a port of call for ships coming from all over the Middle East. Paul had to insert the Christian way of life into a pagan and a very immoral city.

It is actually reported that there is sexual immorality among you, and of a kind that is not found even among pagans; for a man is living with his father's wife. And you are arrogant! Should you not rather have mourned, so that he who has done this would have been removed from among you? For though absent in body, I am present in spirit; and as if present I have already pronounced judgement in the name of the Lord Jesus on the man who has done such a thing. When you are assembled, and my spirit is present with the power of our Lord Jesus, you are to hand this man over to Satan for the destruction of the flesh, so that his spirit may be saved in the day of the Lord.

1 Corinthians 5:1-5

This is also the background of the Sacrament of Penance in the Catholic Church. The Church excludes from communion those who have committed a serious sin. This exclusion in a way is 'handing over to Satan' the sinner, because that man or woman is excluded from the greatest means of grace, Holy Communion. But that exclusion has a positive intention: that the person will repent of their sin and return to the right way. Then, like the Prodigal Son returning home to his father (Lk 15:11-31), that person will be welcomed back into full communion with God and with the Church.

The reason why Paul condemns incest is most important here:

Do you not know that your bodies are members of Christ? Should I therefore take the members of Christ and make them members of a prostitute? Never! Do you not know that whoever is united to a prostitute becomes one body with her? For it is said, 'The two shall be one flesh.' But anyone united to the Lord becomes one spirit with him. Shun fornication! Every sin that a person commits is outside the body; but the fornicator sins against the body itself. Or do you not know that your body is a temple of the Holy Spirit within you, which you have from God, and that you are not your own? For you were bought with a price; therefore glorify God in your body.

1 Corinthians 6:15-20

There, in a nutshell, is the whole of the teaching of the Catholic Church on sex! Let us take the points one by one:

- Sexual intercourse is a sacred act, because thereby two bodies, one male and one female, are united as one body (cf Genesis 2:24, where the man and the woman become 'one flesh'). This is fulfilled in marriage. Paul would have had this Jewish background as he meditated on Genesis. 'One flesh' for the Jewish reader of the Bible would always mean nothing less than marriage, because that union was not merely physical. Rather, the sex act was a sign of a permanent and personal union between male and female, fruitful when God acted to bring forth a child from that union.

- It is quite wrong, therefore, for a man to join himself with a 'prostitute'. This word does not necessarily mean a woman who is paid money for her services! It means most likely any kind of immoral union. A union which is not within marriage destroys the meaning of the sex act, which, as we have said above, is a sign of a union which is permanent between persons, and open to new life. This new life needs the permanent relationship of mother and father to thrive.

- The Christian can never say, 'My body is my own. I can do what I like with it.' On the contrary, the Christian's body is consecrated to the service of God, and to his Son Jesus Christ, who has saved us from our sins and given us the new life of God through his Spirit. The human body cannot ever be offered for mere pleasure, only for union between persons in marriage, according to God's law as expressed in Genesis.

- Finally, sexual sin is serious. Paul says, 'Every sin that a person commits is outside the body; but the fornicator sins against the body itself.' Again, 'fornication' here means most likely any form of sexual immorality. Paul is saying that in committing sexually immoral acts, we as members of the body of Christ are abusing our bodies, which should be 'for the Lord' and not for sin.

Paul is at one with Jesus here. Christ condemned some sins perhaps even more than sexual ones, such as avarice (Mt 6:24) and hypocrisy (Mk 7:6). But we have seen above how seriously Jesus himself took sexual sin, even when only committed in the 'heart' of the adulterer. Sexual sin destroys that 'purity of heart' which Jesus gave as one of his Beatitudes. An act which should be the sign of permanent communion between persons becomes a false sign, because it takes place outside that communion of persons. For Paul, and for the Christian tradition after him, it is wrong to say that illicit sex 'does no harm to anyone'. Rather, it harms the whole person because we are acting against the law of our being as created male and female by God.

Q. But did not Paul prefer celibacy to marriage?

A. Only in his case, and where individual Christians judged that to be best for themselves. Paul's view is very balanced here:

> Now concerning virgins, I have no command of the Lord, but I give my opinion as one who by the Lord's mercy is trustworthy. I think that, in view of the impending crisis, it is well for you to remain as you are. Are you bound to a wife? Do not seek to be free. Are you free from a wife? Do not seek a wife. But if you marry, you do not sin, and if a virgin marries, she does not sin. Yet those who marry will experience distress in this life, and I would spare you that. I mean, brothers and sisters, the appointed time has grown short; from now on, let even those who have wives be as though they had none, and those who mourn as though they were not mourning, and those who rejoice as though they were not rejoicing, and those who buy as though they had no possessions.
>
> 1 Corinthians 7:25-30

Some think that Paul was expecting the end of the world to come soon. No doubt some Christians thought so in his day, as they do today! But there is no real evidence that Paul did expect the end of the world quickly. Rather, Christians were living in a world which would soon be systematically persecuting them, sending them to death in public games, eaten by lions. Paul is saying, 'When in doubt, stay as you are!'

Q. But surely his view of marriage was jaundiced, seen only as a remedy for concupiscence?

A. The offending text is as follows:

> I wish that all were as I myself am. But each has a particular gift from God, one having one kind and another a different kind. To the unmarried and the widows I say that it is well for them to remain unmarried as I am. But if they are not practising self-control, they should marry. For it is better to marry than to be aflame with passion.
>
> 1 Corinthians 7:7-9

That looks as if Paul is treating marriage as second best, only for those with insufficient self-control to remain celibate. But it may be that the background of this text was that a number of Corinthian Christians were reacting to the immorality around them by saying that marriage and sex were wrong. We know that there were such movements later in the history of the Church, people called Gnostics, pedaling a superior kind of knowledge which disdained the body. In this context, what Paul says above is more positive. He is saying, 'If you can remain celibate, that is fine. But if you cannot, for heaven's sake marry. There is nothing wrong in that, contrary to what some of you are saying.'

We will have to return to Paul later in this book when we discuss the whole question of divorce and remarriage.

But, in order to see a more positive side to Paul's view of marriage, we must end here by quoting Ephesians. Some scholars doubt whether this letter was actually written by Paul. But no one doubts that it expresses his spirit, even if the scribe was someone else continuing in the tradition of the great apostle:

> Husbands, love your wives, just as Christ loved the church and gave himself up for her, in order to make her holy by cleansing her with the washing of water by the word, so as to present the church to himself in splendor, without a spot or wrinkle or anything of the kind – yes, so that she may be holy and without blemish. In the same way, husbands should love their wives as they do their own bodies. He who loves his wife loves himself.
>
> Ephesians 5:25-28

Feminists will note that the imagery is patriarchal, as one would expect in the Judaism of the time! But remember that Paul is providing an image. The male and the female represent an image of Christ (male) and his Church (female). This image will enrich the whole tradition of thinking about Christian marriage in the centuries after St Paul.

6

The Church's authority

Q. Why should the Church tell me what to do and what not to do in bed?

A. Because the Church tells us what God says. And God, who knows all the secrets of our hearts, has every right to tell us what to do and what not to do in bed, as anywhere else! As Paul said to the Thessalonian Christians: 'We also constantly give thanks to God for this, that when you received the word of God that you heard from us, you accepted it not as a human word but as what it really is, God's word, which is also at work in you believers'(1 Thess 2:13).

We believe that what the Church teaches is God's revelation. That is why it has authority. Over the past five chapters, we have argued that there are the following springs of morality. These are all God's revelation to us as human beings:

- **The Natural Law**: That is, God's Word within our hearts, revealing what is right according to our nature. Our conscience then tells us what is right and wrong; but that is God speaking to us.

- **The Ten Commandments**: That is God's Word origi-
  nally given to the people of God in the Old Testament.
  This clarifies what is in the Natural Law. Our con-
  science could be erroneous, particularly due to Original
  Sin. The Ten Commandments make it clear what that
  Moral Law is.

- **The Teaching of Jesus**: Jesus, we believe, is the Word
  of God made flesh, true God and true Man. He left us
  his own revelation. This reaffirmed the Natural Law
  and the Ten Commandments. Jesus also gave us the
  true interpretation of the Law, and by saving us by his
  death and resurrection and the gift of the Holy Spirit
  gave us the grace to follow the right way.

- **The New Testament**: Particularly in the letters of St
  Paul, we see the Natural Law, the Ten Commandments
  and the teaching of Jesus confirmed. Paul emphasises
  that we are now all members of the body of Christ, and
  need to live accordingly in the Spirit.

All this is 'what it really is, God's Word' and not merely
some human opinion. That is why we must follow the
Church's teaching; because it is God's teaching!

Q. **But not all that the Catholic Church teaches about
sex today can be found in the Bible, the Ten Commandments, the teaching of Jesus or the New Testament. For
instance, contraception is not explicitly forbidden in the
Bible, yet the Church says that is wrong. How is this
justified?**

A. We believe as Catholics that the Word of God, his
revelation to us, is contained not only in the Bible but in
unwritten Tradition handed on. Books, however holy, cannot contain all Christian faith and morals. There is the need
for the living voice of Tradition. The new Catechism quotes

the Second Vatican Council's Constitution on Divine Revelation here:

> 81 '*Sacred Scripture* is the speech of God as it is put down in writing under the breath of the Holy Spirit.'
>
> 'And [Holy] *Tradition* transmits in its entirety the Word of God which has been entrusted to the apostles by Christ the Lord and the Holy Spirit. It transmits it to the successors of the apostles so that, enlightened by the Spirit of truth, they may faithfully preserve, expound and spread it abroad by their preaching.'
>
> 82 As a result the Church, to whom the transmission and interpretation of Revelation is entrusted, 'does not derive her certainty about all revealed truths from the holy Scriptures alone. Both Scripture and Tradition must be accepted and honoured with equal sentiments of devotion and reverence.'

St Paul speaks of this living tradition in his letters. 'So then, brothers and sisters, stand firm and hold fast to the traditions that you were taught by us, either by word of mouth or by our letter (2 Thess 2:15). Paul expected those Christians to follow not only what was written, but what had been handed on by him by word of mouth.

One example of such moral tradition is the Church's teaching on abortion. Killing unborn children is not condemned explicitly as a sin in the Old Testament. But there is an early Christian document, first or second century not part of the Scriptures but part of the Church Tradition, a book called the *Didaché* (Teaching) *of the Twelve Apostles.* This book condemns both abortion and the horrible practice in the Roman Empire of leaving infants out in the cold to see if they would be tough enough to survive.

Scholars consider that the *Didaché is* here reflecting Jewish tradition, handed on to Christians through Jewish converts to Christianity. The Old Testament had a living tradition as well as the New Testament. After all, the first Christians were all Jews; we would be surprised if the living tradition of Judaism were not handed on to Christians through those Jewish Christians.

The Ten Commandments only say, 'You shall not kill'. They do not specify the matter further. Yet it is clear that the Old Testament did allow some killing: in battle, and also as a punishment for crimes, particularly against the Ten Commandments. The commandments were originally legal obligations as well as moral obligations. What was forbidden was murder, the direct and deliberate killing of the innocent.

Thus it would be quite logical to assume that in the Old Testament tradition, long before Christianity came, abortion was condemned as the direct and deliberate killing of the innocent.

In any case, from that time onwards, Christian tradition has always condemned abortion as a serious sin. The Church has interpreted with its authority the meaning of the fifth commandment, 'You shall not kill' as referring also to unborn children.

Q. But who decides as to what is in the Tradition or not?

A. That is a fair question! It is similar to asking who has the authority to interpret the Bible. The Catholic Church always insists that private interpretation is not sufficient. There is the need for the teaching authority (the Magisterium) of the Church, to decide in difficult cases. The Magisterium, the Church's Senate if you like, consists of the bishops of the Catholic Church throughout the world in communion with the Pope, who is the successor of Peter. As the Catechism says:

85 'The task of giving an authentic interpretation of the Word of God, whether in its written form or in the form

of Tradition, has been entrusted to the living teaching office of the Church alone. Its authority in this matter is exercised in the name of Jesus Christ.' This means that the task of interpretation has been entrusted to the bishops in communion with the successor of Peter, the Bishop of Rome.

86 'Yet this Magisterium is not superior to the Word of God, but is its servant. It teaches only what has been handed on to it. At the divine command and with the help of the Holy Spirit, it listens to this devotedly, guards it with dedication and expounds it faithfully. All that it proposes for belief as being divinely revealed is drawn from this single deposit of faith.'

87 Mindful of Christ's words to his apostles: 'He who hears you, hears me', the faithful receive with docility the teachings and directives that their pastors give them in different forms.

Q. But how do we know that what the Magisterium proposes to us for our belief is true?

A. By the fact that Christ handed on to the Church a share in his own infallibility, with the help of the Holy Spirit. This infallibility would enable the Church to be guided into all truth. Not all Church teaching is infallible; but even where it is not, it is still good for our guidance, and should be obeyed. Jesus said to his apostles: 'When the Spirit of truth comes, he will guide you into all the truth; for he will not speak on his own, but will speak whatever he hears, and he will declare to you the things that are to come' (Jn 16:13).

This gift of infallibility enables the Church to make the right decisions in matters of faith and morals, so to hand on the true teaching of Christ. The Catechism tells us:

890 The mission of the Magisterium is linked to the definitive nature of the covenant established by God with his people in Christ. It is this Magisterium's task to preserve God's people from deviations and defections and to guarantee them the objective possibility of professing the true faith without error. Thus, the pastoral duty of the Magisterium is aimed at seeing to it that the People of God abides in the truth that liberates. To fulfil this service, Christ endowed the Church's shepherds with the charism of infallibility in matters of faith and morals. The exercise of this charism takes several forms:

891 'The Roman Pontiff, head of the college of bishops, enjoys this infallibility in virtue of his office, when, as supreme pastor and teacher of all the faithful – who confirms his brethren in the faith – he proclaims by a definitive act a doctrine pertaining to faith or morals... The infallibility promised to the Church is also present in the body of bishops when, together with Peter's successor, they exercise the supreme Magisterium', above all in an Ecumenical Council. When the Church through its supreme Magisterium proposes a doctrine 'for belief as being divinely revealed', and as the teaching of Christ, the definitions 'must be adhered to with the obedience of faith'. This infallibility extends as far as the deposit of divine Revelation itself.

Q. But surely this teaching must change with changing times?

A. Yes and no. Doctrines such as the Trinity, that God is Three Persons in One, and the Incarnation, that Jesus Christ is true God and Man, will never change; yet even here, there is always development in understanding of those mysteries of faith.

Even more is this the case with moral matters. The

Church has always defended the right of states to self-defence, even to the point of killing unjust attackers (cf *Catechism of the Catholic Church* 2266). Up to recently, the stance of pacifism was not in any way encouraged by the Church, except insofar as those in Holy Orders were forbidden to take up arms, just as they were forbidden to run a business! But, since the Second Vatican Council, the Church has praised those who choose the option of refusing to kill and so to become 'peacemakers' as commended in the Beatitudes by Jesus.

But – and this is a big 'but' – the Church can never change its teaching over what has been stated by the Magisterium as an act which is intrinsically evil', that is to say, an act which can never in any circumstances be right. The clearest example of this is blasphemy. It can never be right to blaspheme, to curse God. This can never change, because it is in Latin *per se malum,* that is, evil in itself as an act. It can never be right yesterday, today or tomorrow.

The *Catechism of the Catholic Church* gives us a list of such acts:

> 1756 It is therefore an error to judge the morality of human acts by considering only the intention that inspires them or the circumstances (environment, social pressure, duress or emergency, etc.) which supply their context. There are acts which, in and of themselves, independently of circumstances and intentions, are always gravely illicit by reason of their object; such as blasphemy and perjury, murder and adultery. One may not do evil so that good may result from it.

In 1968, Pope Paul VI caused a furore throughout the world when he stated in his encyclical *Humanae Vitae* (Of Human Life) that contraceptive sex, even within marriage, was an example of an 'intrinsically evil' act, and so could never be right. The consequences of that famous (to some infamous) encyclical are still with us. To that we now turn, in the second part of our book. Having considered the fundamental principles of Catholic sexual morality, we now consider some practical consequences in terms of human activity.

7

What are our sex organs for?

As human beings, we are spiritual and material, soul and body. Our soul is not separate from our body, even if it transcends the body, and will live when our body is dead. In fact, we can never act purely spiritually. Our minds, our wills, can only act through our bodies. Our bodies are miracles in themselves, the unique work of our Creator:

> For it was you who formed my inward parts; you knit me together in my mother's womb.
> I praise you, for I am fearfully and wonderfully made.
> Wonderful are your works; that I know very well.
> My frame was not hidden from you, when I was being made in secret,
> intricately woven in the depths of the earth.
> Your eyes beheld my unformed substance.
> In your book were written all the days that were formed for me, when none of them as yet existed.
>
> Psalm 139:13-16

We do not believe that we are the work of a mindless and chance evolution, but of an infinite Intelligence, even if we have evolved as part of a creative process. We have each been created with love and care by that infinitely loving

Mind. Each part of our body has its own function, and each is much more complicated and well made than the most expensive car. And, as we have seen in the early chapters of this book, everything we have and are as humans is there made for a purpose, to serve our final end, which is eternal happiness with God.

Our mouths take in food, to give us strength and health. Our mouths also enable us to communicate with other human beings, to encourage others in their difficulties, and to sing God's praises. Our mouths also, however, can eat or drink too much, or take drugs harmful to our bodies, even destructive of our life. Our mouths can also do great harm to others through angry words or by telling lies about people.

Our vocation as Christians is to use our bodies for the glory of God and to help our neighbour. This does not mean that our bodies should not serve our own well-being. Having given us a body, God wishes us to take care of that body as our most precious possession, given by him to us on trust. But it does mean that our bodies have been given to us for a purpose; and our happiness consists not in doing what we like with our own bodies, but serving that eternal purpose for which we were created.

St Paul puts it this way: 'Therefore, do not let sin exercise dominion in your mortal bodies, to make you obey their passions. No longer present your members to sin as instruments of wickedness, but present yourselves to God as those who have been brought from death to life, and present your members to God as instruments of righteousness' (Rom 6:12-13).

Our sexual organs – the man's penis and scrotum, the woman's vagina, womb, and breasts – are made equally wonderfully as the rest of our bodies. They are unique in that they form the object of sexual desire, as well as performing functions for which they were designed. They serve the unique purpose of communicating life, of procreating other human beings.

There is a paradox here. St Augustine somewhat cynically observed, *interfaeces et urinam nascitur* (We were born between the faeces and the urine). That makes us humble in realising that we are dust, and to dust we shall return (*see* Gen 3:19). This paradox may also have led St Paul to write the following about the various members of the body:

> The members of the body that seem to be weaker are indispensable, and those members of the body that we think less honourable we clothe with greater honour, and our less respectable members are treated with greater respect; whereas our more respectable members do not need this. But God has so arranged the body, giving the greater honour to the inferior member, that there may be no dissension within the body, but the members may have the same care for one another.
>
> 1 Corinthians 12:22-25

The point that we have been making all through this book is that we may not use our bodily functions purely for pleasure, but only for the purpose for which they were created, to serve our final end of eternal happiness with God. We may distinguish here 'pleasure' from 'happiness'. God intends our final happiness, and that includes legitimate pleasure, and pleasure from our bodily functions, from eating and drinking, from sex. But pleasure which detracts from our final happiness is false pleasure, and is an evil, a sin.

We enjoy good food and drink. God wants us to do so, because it is using the bodily functions he has provided for a good purpose, our health and welfare. God makes eating and drinking a pleasure in order to encourage us to build up our health and strength. In eating and drinking, and enjoying eating and drinking, we are in harmony with the will of our loving Creator.

On the other hand, eating and drinking can be harmful

either to our bodies or to the welfare of others. Gluttony or drunkenness can harm our bodies, make fools of us during a party, or deprive others of the food and drink they need, if too much of the family budget is used for booze. The Church also encourages people to deprive themselves voluntarily of food, in order to provide for those desperately short of the necessities of life, as well as to promote the spiritual effects of self-control in the person fasting.

The bodily function of eating, therefore, has a spiritual function as well as a purely physical function, when forming part of a human activity. The act of eating and drinking can serve our social and our spiritual life, or be detrimental to it. But the spiritual function of eating and drinking is not divorced from the right use of the natural function of eating. On the contrary, to use the body the way nature wishes it is also to serve the higher purpose of human life and of life with God.

What is the purpose of human sexual organs? Their reproductive purpose is served by a unitive act between male and female; by the insertion of the male penis, hardened by the pleasure of the act of sexual love, into the female vagina, where seed is deposited in the woman's body. The male semen will attempt to fertilise the ovum; and when success occurs and the ovum is fertilised, a new human life is created, formed in the womb of the mother. As with eating, where a function which enables humans to live and grow is also a means of human society, so what is a biological mechanism for promoting life is also a unique means of communion between male and female.

It is worth pausing to reflect on the fact that God need not have made the sexual organs this way. He could have created us so that a child was born quite in isolation from any act between humans. It is clear that he created us this way so that a new human life could be born from the love of man and woman. Our mouths, as we have seen, can be instruments of human communication, as well as means of consuming material food. So also, our sexual organs, as well as biologically speaking serving procreation, promote a loving relationship. This man and woman should then bring that child into the world in love. That child should be nurtured in love, and should in turn provide a further bond of love between the man and the woman. The family then should grow in love and fidelity to each other. This is what the sexual organs are 'for' in the whole plan of God. The act of sexual intercourse, therefore, has a human and spiritual purpose, as well as a purely physical one of providing means of reproduction. It unites man and woman physically in love, in order to cause the human family to grow in that same love and intimacy.

This is precisely what we call marriage, as the *Catechism of the Catholic Church* states:

> 2361 'Sexuality, by means of which man and woman give themselves to one another through the acts which are proper and exclusive to spouses, is not something simply biological, but concerns the innermost being of the human person as such. It is realised in a truly human way only if it is an integral part of the love by which a man and woman commit themselves totally to one another until death.'

> 2362 The acts in marriage by which the intimate and chaste union of the spouses takes place are noble and honourable; the truly human performance of these acts fosters the self-giving they signify, and enriches the spouses in joy and gratitude.' Sexuality is a source of joy and pleasure:

> The Creator himself... established that in the [generative] function, spouses should experience pleasure and enjoyment of body and spirit. Therefore, the spouses do nothing evil in seeking this pleasure and enjoyment. They accept what the Creator has intended for them. At the same time, spouses should

71

know how to keep themselves within the limits of just moderation (Pius XII).

But, as with any other bodily function, the deeper spiritual purpose of the sexual organs cannot be separated from, and cannot contradict, their natural function. The biological serves the purpose of married love. That purpose, as we have said, flows from observation as to how the child is born, by union between male and female. If we ask 'What are the sexual organs for.' we can only reply that God has given us those sexual organs in order to unite a man with the one woman he has chosen and with her agreement to become one flesh. As with eating, a physical activity becomes the means of spiritual bonding:

> 1643 'Conjugal love involves a totality, in which all the elements of the person enter '– appeal of the body and instinct, power of feeling and affectivity, aspiration of the spirit and of will. It aims at a deeply personal unity, a unity that, beyond union in one flesh, leads to forming one heart and soul; it demands *indissolubility* and *faithfulness* in definitive mutual giving; and it is open to *fertility* . In a word it is a question of the normal characteristics of all natural conjugal love, but with a new significance which not only purifies and strengthens them, but raises them to the extent of making them the expression of specifically Christian values.'

Q. But surely we can eat for pleasure, without thinking too much about the function of providing health for the body? What, then, is wrong in using our sexual organs purely for pleasure?

A. We often perform actions without thinking too much of their purpose, but simply enjoy them. That is true, particularly where eating is concerned. But, when eating, we do not *exclude the possibility* of that eating following its natural course to provide us with nourishment. This point is well made by Mgr A.N. Gilbey in his clear presentation of the Catholic faith (A.N. Gilbey: *We Believe, A Simple Commentary on The Catechism of Christian Doctrine Approved by the Archbishops and Bishops of England and Wales* Valetta, Malta, Progress Press, 1994, pp. 221-2).

> Here is a comparison which may help to make clear the wickedness of getting the pleasure of an act whilst excluding the possibility of the consequence for which that act is intended by Almighty God. The Romans, we are told – though it is hard for us to imagine the mentality that allowed them to act in that way – ate and drank till they could hold no more and then made themselves sick in order to have the pleasure of eating and drinking again.
>
> That is the perfect parallel to what we do when we exercise our sexual gifts and yet exclude the possibility of their resulting in the purpose for which Almighty God has intended them. Food and drink are given to us so that we may replenish our bodily strength. So long as we are not excluding the possibility of its nourishing us, it is right to take pleasure in drinking. There is nothing wrong or sinful about it. When we start eating and drinking solely for pleasure, as in the Roman example I have given you, the attempt to obtain the pleasure while excluding the purpose for which it is given is sinful.

Mgr Gilbey outlines this fundamental principle of Catholic sexuality as well as I have seen it:

> In giving us the gift of procreation, Almighty God has given us a share in this uniquely and specifically divine role of calling things into being. So the gift of sex is something sublime and sacred. Nothing could be a greater distortion of the Christian view of sex than to consider it something low, degrading and unworthy. It is not; it is something absolutely sublime.

But like every gift which Almighty God has given us, it has to be exercised in accordance with His will and purpose. Rightly exercised, it is something positively sanctifying and is in no way sinful.

This is true of all God's gifts, whether they are gifts of mind or body, intellect or physical strength or beauty. They may all be used according to His will and purpose, in which case our use of them is something that helps to sanctify us, or they can be used contrary to His will and purpose, in which case our use of them takes us away from Him and is the occasion of sin.

That is particularly plain with gifts of the mind. The use of the mind to discover truth, to discover God Himself, is plainly something sanctifying. Its use apart from Him, in opposition to Him, is something which leads to that root of all sins, the sin of pride. It can be used to very evil purpose indeed.

Our sexual and procreative gifts are given to us so that we may bring life into being. Not only that, but when life has been brought into being, we should exercise the conservative role by rearing that life in the knowledge and love of Almighty God. Always remember that you cannot separate procreation from education – the bringing of life into being from the nurturing of that life. It is a double role which cannot be divided any more than the creative and conservative power of Almighty God can be divided.

Used for its proper end and purpose, sex is a holy and a sanctifying thing. Used to the exclusion of its proper purpose – procreation and education, which are so inextricably united – it becomes an occasion of sin. We are using a gift of Almighty God for a purpose other than that for which it was intended.

You will see, if you apply that yardstick, that every sin of a sexual character derives its malice from excluding one or other of those purposes. Plainly masturbation excludes the very possibility of procreation taking place; as do homosexual acts and the practice of artificial birth-control. Adultery and fornication exclude the possibility of bringing up the fruits of such a union within the framework of a Christian family and it is only in such a framework that the conservative responsibilities of our sexual gifts can be fulfilled. Every one of the abuses of our sexual gifts derives its malice, as I have said, from excluding the possibility of procreation or the possibility of education within a Christian context. And that is why they are sinful, not because the activity itself is sinful. It is not sinful at all: used properly, it is sanctifying.

We would wish to add that our procreative organs are given in order that their procreative function should be joined with the spiritual nature of the human person in love being generated between husband and wife in marriage, love of neighbour as well as of Almighty God. But Mgr Gilbey is still right in insisting that we cannot act morally if we act against the purpose of our sexual organs; any more than we can act morally if we act against the God-ordained purpose of any part of our bodies.

Q. What of those couples who cannot have children? Their sexual organs cannot procreate. How, in your view, could they legitimately have sex without procreation?

A. Again, a couple who might be sterile are not positively excluding procreation when they have sex together. Therefore, they can use their sexual organs to gain that intimacy of communion with each other, even when procreation is excluded physically. The Catechism says:

> 1654 Spouses to whom God has not granted children can nevertheless have a conjugal life full of meaning, in both human and Christian terms. Their marriage can

radiate a fruitfulness of charity, of hospitality and of sacrifice.

It is worth remembering that the Holy Family of Jesus, Mary and Joseph did not conceive a child from their own physical union. Yet their life, with the Son of God Jesus born of the Virgin Mary, was happy and fulfilled. Perhaps here is a model for couples unable to conceive, perhaps fulfilling their desire for parenthood with adopted children, or even with each other if children are denied.

8

Contraception

Q. Surely, Pope Paul VI in 1968 made a big mistake in condemning all forms of contraception. Why did he reject the findings of the Commission he set up?

A. In 1968, Paul VI issued the famous (to some infamous) encyclical *Humanae Vitae* (Cf Human Life). Pope John XXIII had set up a Commission to discuss the whole question of contraception, which up to then had been condemned as seriously sinful by the Church's ethical tradition. Could there be a change in this matter? Particularly regarding the new anovalent pill, it was argued that this was not necessarily contraceptive, but simply making the woman's safe period safer.

Pope Paul VI caused an uproar throughout the world's media in rejecting the findings of the majority of the Commission, who said that the pill could be morally acceptable, while other forms of contraception were immoral. The Pope argued that the Church's tradition must stand. All forms of contraception, including the pill (which was in fact contraceptive) were morally unacceptable. Only the 'safe period', that period during a woman's menstrual cycle where she was infertile, could be used with moral legitimacy for sexual intercourse within marriage.

Clearly, the Pope had agonised long about this himself.

He was under a great deal of pressure from all kinds of groups to effect a change. The Second Vatican Council had just finished, in 1965, a great reforming Council where the 'progressives', the forward-looking element in the Church, had won many changes. Most noticeable immediately was the permission granted to celebrate the Mass in the local vernacular language. It was no longer mandatory always to celebrate Mass in Latin, as it had been in the Western Church throughout the world. Could not there be a change in sexual ethics also, which would bring the Church into line with the modern world?

On the other hand, the Pope could not be bound by the findings of a Commission. A commission, whether of the Church or of a government, is only consultative, not authoritative. The Pope, as the successor of Peter and the head of the Church's Magisterium, decided that the Church's teaching could not be changed.

To understand why, we must go back to the chapter where we considered the Church's authority. There is nothing explicitly condemning contraception in the Bible, although it may be that a certain Onan in the Old Testament, who spilled his semen on the ground whenever he went into his brother's wife, (Gen 38:9) and who as a result was 'displeasing to the Lord' (Gen 38:10),was condemned by God for a form of contraception, *coitus interruptus.* However, other scholars argued that Onan displeased God because he refused to follow the Levitical law that, if a man died, his brother was obliged to have intercourse with the dead man's wife to make sure she was not childless.

What was more certain, and which certainly influenced the Pope more, was that the Church's tradition had universally condemned contraception throughout its history. Popes had reiterated this condemnation. Priests in the confessional had always treated contraceptive intercourse as a serious sin. In fact, all Christian Churches, and the Jewish and Moslem faiths, were equally sure in their condemnation of this practice. The Pope was convinced that the living Tradition of the

Church had always condemned contraception, and that this could not be changed by any human authority. Even a famous theologian, Dr Hans Küng, who dissented from this teaching, had to admit that Church Tradition was clear as to the moral unacceptability of contraception. He simply argued that the doctrine of the infallibility of the Church's teaching authority had to be abandoned! But then, of course, the Church loses its doctrinal and moral authority given to it by Christ himself, and abandons its commission to preach the truth of the Gospel with certainty. The Catholic Church would then cease to be the Catholic Church.

The Catechism summarises the argument concerning the moral unacceptability of contraception:

> 2366 Fecundity (i.e. fruitfulness) is a gift, an *end of marriage*, for conjugal love naturally tends to be fruitful. A child does not come from outside as something added on to the mutual love of the spouses, but springs from the very heart of that mutual giving, as its fruit and fulfilment. So the Church, which 'is on the side of life' teaches that 'each and every marriage act must remain open to the transmission of life'. 'This particular doctrine, expounded on numerous occasions by the Magisterium, is based on the inseparable connection, established by God, which man on his own initiative may not break, between the unitive significance and the procreative significance which are both inherent to the marriage act.'

The Church here argues, as we did in the last chapter, in relation to the whole purpose of the act of marriage. The Church looked back to the biblical encouragement to humans to procreate: 'God blessed them, and God said to them, "Be fruitful and multiply, and fill the earth and subdue it; and have dominion over the fish of the sea and over the birds of the air and over every living thing that moves upon the earth"' (Gen 1:28).

But the roots of the Church's teaching go back even before Christianity, to Stoic philosophy in ancient Greece. This philosophy was taken up by Augustine of Hippo of the sixth century AD. Augustine argued that 'as the eye is to see, so the generative organs are to generate with'. Thus, the classical argument goes, to engage in sexual intercourse without orientation to procreation is therefore 'against nature' and wrong.

Many theologians and philosophers today will attack this principle as 'simplistic', 'biologistic' and 'mechanistic'. There are more profound reasons at the basis of sexuality in Christian terms than simply procreation, as have been outlined above regarding the unitive side of procreation. But it still remains true that the Church in its moral teaching about sexuality has in no way surrendered this necessary principle, going back to the roots of Greek and Gentile Christianity together with Augustine of Hippo, that a sexual act to be morally right must not deliberately prevent conception, but must be open to life within marriage.

Q. But how could Pope Paul VI continue to forbid contraception when he accepted the 'safe period' to limit families?

A. This is the reason given by the Pope himself in the encyclical *Humanae Vitae* why contraception is wrong, but the use of the infertile period can be acceptable:

> These two situations are essentially different. In the first (the use of the infertile period) the spouses legitimately use a faculty that is given by nature; in the second case,(i.e. contraception), the spouses impede the order of generation (*ordo generationis*) from completing its own natural processes. (Translation of *Humanae Vitae* by J.E. Smith, *Humanae Vitae. A Generation Later,* Washington, Catholic University of America Press, 1991, p. 281)

This is a principle which works throughout Catholic morality: that we may not do evil that good may come, if that act is 'intrinsically evil'. But we can allow nature to take its course in the right circumstances. Thus a dying person who is old and who would suffer a great deal in treatment could refuse an operation which only offered fairly low chances of success. In the same way, the Pope argues, the use of the infertile period is simply allowing nature to take its course. The couple, while not seeking to conceive in this period, are at least open to the transmission of life if the Almighty in his Providence decides to bestow new life. This would even be true regarding a couple who are married, yet who are physically sterile. If they had intercourse together, even though fertility would be impossible, their intercourse would not be a sin. They would not be *preventing* fertility, but again letting nature take its course.

Q. But the safe period is not really safe, is it?

A. The increasing number of married couples who use what they now call, Natural Family Planning (NFP) find it very safe. In fact, family planning groups say that, if properly used, it is in fact safer than artificial contraception. This fact is now admitted even by those who promote contraceptives. The real problem today with all forms of Natural Family Planning is that they will not prevent sexually transmitted diseases. Thus NFP is very much a method for married couples whose sexuality is exclusive to themselves, who obey God's law of sexuality; not for those millions today who, influenced by media and commercial propaganda, are sexually promiscuous.

Provided that you are properly taught, there is no doubt that NFP is among the most effective forms of family planning available today, and unlike the others in its effectiveness league, it has no unpleasant medical side-effects.

And there is a continuous debate about the medical dangers of the Pill and of the Intra-uterine Device (IUD). In general, medical evidence which tends to draw attention to the dangers of contraceptives is played down by interested parties.

Put simply, married couples who use it say NFP is a way of understanding our fertility, and then using our understanding to plan our family. It's a way of learning the signs which tell us about the menstrual cycle which every fertile woman (and so every fertile couple) has, and using the signs to achieve or to avoid pregnancy. It's a scientific system of observing and interpreting these signs. And it is not that difficult. Mother Teresa of Calcutta was successful in teaching mothers in extreme poverty NFP in the Third World.

You certainly do not need to have a regular cycle to use NFP; you can learn at any stage of your fertile life (including while breastfeeding – in fact, couples in the process of forming their families can also rely on a natural period of infertility during breastfeeding, if they know how to recognise the signs of returning fertility). And you do not need to be super-intelligent. Learning NFP is rather like learning to ride a bike, or to swim: it becomes easy with practice!

At a deeper level, it's the key to living and loving as a married couple, in harmony with the way God created us, and to making our sexuality the heart of our married love.

Q. I have heard the objection that the use of Natural Family Planning makes the act of love between married couples unnatural. When they feel like having sex together, they find that just at that moment the 'charts' tell them that they will conceive, and so must abstain. Is this not bad for their married relationship?

A. Not if they understand the value of their fertility. Our fertility is God's personal invitation to us to join him in the creation of a new human being, who will live for all eternity. This is one of his greatest and most awe-inspiring gifts to married couples, and it has a profound effect on our attitude to our children and to family life.

82

But sometimes, the time is not right to conceive a child, and we need to refrain from intercourse for a short while in each cycle. In these times we don't stop loving each other, of course: indeed, sometimes it seems that these are the most loving times. Each couple develop their own vocabulary of love for these times, and each couple find out how many ways of loving there are. Then, when the waiting is over, there is the 'honeymoon' phase, when our sexual intercourse can truly be the summit of the experience of loving we have built up throughout the whole cycle.

Q. What is the most effective form of Natural Family Planning? Do we have to get into complicated charts and tests? What about the new computer method we have all heard about?

A. Note that the Church teaches that there must be serious reasons for the couple to use any method of Natural Family Planning. There are two main methods used today – the Ovulation or Billings Method (OM) and the Symptothermal Method (STM). Most statistics indicate that the STM is a little more effective, but they are both about as effective as the Pill.

The newer device in the field is the Persona fertility monitor. It takes less learning to use, but on the other hand the effectiveness levels quoted are not as good as those of the STM or OM, and from what we have seen it is not as easy to use in times of changing fertility (like the menopause and after childbirth).

Q. Natural Family Planning is fine if you are both committed Catholics. But what if only one of the couple wishes to use NFP and the other is firmly set against the idea?

A. NFP isn't only for Catholics! It's used by all sorts of people for all sorts of reasons: some to do with religious beliefs, others simply because it is natural and fits with a more ecological lifestyle. The question really is why one spouse is against it. A couple in this situation really need to talk to an NFP teaching couple who can help them understand fully what NFP is about at all levels. At the end of the day, if the values of marriage are important enough to them, then the way NFP fits with and builds up those values – whereas unnatural methods actually erode them – is likely to lead them at least to try it. And most people who try it stay with it!

On the other hand, we must admit that often the spouse who wants to avoid using contraceptives is unable to persuade his or her partner, and a moral dilemma is created. We will be dealing with such moral dilemmas in the next chapter, when we deal with sin, forgiveness and responsibility.

It does seem, however (and the Church has not condemned this view), that it is morally permissible to use contraceptives against rape. This ties up with a terrible case we all heard of in the sixties when a group of nuns in the Congo were raped. The Vatican seemed to say that these sisters could use contraceptives in such a situation, but if a child was conceived it could not be aborted.

How does that make sense? Remember the illustration we used in the last chapter about the Romans? Their gluttony was so extreme that they gorged themselves with food and then went outside to vomit. They wanted the pleasure of eating while depriving nature of the natural purpose of that eating, which is to nourish the body. Mgr Gilby used a parallel argument for the morality of contraception. He argued that it was precisely the same serious misuse of a God-given faculty to have the pleasure of the sexual act while preventing its natural purpose, which is procreation.

Now, a person who is being force-fed would be morally justified in vomiting out that food and drink, if he or she wished, and if the force-feeding were itself unjust. We have such a case in Scripture. A Maccabeean martyr was being force-fed pork, which was forbidden food in the Old Testament. As he went to his martyr's death, he spat out that forbidden food (2 Macc 6:18-19).

Similarly, some moral theologians would argue that it would be morally justified for one being raped to defend oneself by using contraceptives. But it would not be right to abort a child conceived as a result of that violent sexual act; because that unborn child is entirely innocent and so has individually the right to life. And there could be some situations even within marriage where intercourse would be unjustifiably forced upon one of the couple by the other; although cases like this should be discussed with a marriage counsellor, best of all a Catholic Marriage Advisory Council counsellor. 'Conjugal rights' are not absolute!

Q. Condoms are often used as a protection against infection and even possibly death, as in the case of the huge spread of AIDS. Why does the Church condemn the use of contraceptives in this case?

A. The principle applies here that we cannot do evil in order that good may come. If the person did not have intercourse, then the disease would not spread.

Q. How do I find out about Natural Family Planning?

A. You can contact David and Louise Aldred at 44 Park St, Beeston, Nottingham NG9 1DF, or by email at cclgb@aldred.demon.co.uk. My thanks are due to David and Louise for helping me write this chapter. They have had five children, all wanted, and have used nothing other than NFP! Alternatively, your Diocesan Marriage and Family Commission should be able to put you in touch with NFP teachers in your area.

Q. Put it this way. Could you not argue that a married couple may occasionally use contraception, but that

does not destroy the possibility of having children when you consider their marriage as a whole? What is wrong with that?

A. Many of those within the papal commission, and of course many outside it, attempted to use a particular version of what was called the 'principle of totality'. It was argued that, while the totality of the married relationship was open to procreation, then individual acts within marriage could be contraceptive. But, as Dr Janet Smith points out in *Humanae Vitae: A Generation Love*, this argument just will not do. It does not work in other areas of morality, for instance in relation to racial discrimination: 'Restaurant owners may open on occasion to serving blacks, but on occasion not. Could they argue that the 'totality' of their acts are open to integration? They may also argue that the good of the restaurant requires such occasional discrimination, otherwise they would not get enough business to stay open (*op.cit.,* pp. 92-3).

Janet Smith argues that in no way would we allow this argument to stand as a justification for racial discrimination. She extends this principle to demolish the parallel argument from totality regarding sexual ethics:

> To put this question even more squarely in the context of marriage, why do all the acts of intercourse between spouses need to be loving? If the totality of these acts are loving, why would it not be permissible that some of them be the product of force? The Church teaches that acts of sexual intercourse must be with one's spouse. Do spouses need always to be faithful? Could not someone use the principle of totality to argue that an occasional affair might help the whole of the marriage?
> (*op.cit.,* pp. 92-3)

These moral scenarios presented here by Dr Smith are in no way fanciful. Many couples today argue precisely in this way. Some are openly accepting that their spouse might occasionally have an affair. One thing is quite clear. Whether or not we accept the teaching of *Humanae Vitae* or not, it is easy to see how Pope Paul VI was issuing a prophetic warning in 1968 which has been amply fulfilled in the following decades:

> 17 Responsible individuals will quickly see the truth of the Church's teaching [about contraception] if they consider what consequences will follow from the methods of contraception and the reasons given [*vias rationesque*] for the use of contraception. They first should consider how easy it will be (for many) to justify behaviour leading to marital infidelity or to a gradual weakening in the discipline of morals.
>
> (Janet Smith's translation *op.cit.,* pp. 285-86)

This hardly needs any demonstration today. With broken marriages, hundreds of thousands of abortions, condoms even given out to primary school children, the Pope's words have been verified millions of times over. In the sixties, it was married couples who were most insistent upon their right to contraception. But as everyone knows, huge numbers of contraceptives are sold to the unmarried, those in a 'relationship' and to homosexuals. The condom market would not survive on its sales to married couples alone. All admit that the use of the contraceptive has totally changed people's sexual mores, from within the procreative relationship of the family to being a cheap thrill at a few pence a time bought from the slot machine at the local pub loo.

9

What is chastity?

Q. If what you say is right, and people decide to follow the teaching of the Catholic Church, then there will be less sex and more chastity. But what is the advantage? What problem is there with a little bit of casual sex?

A. An ancient Father of the Church, Theophilus of Antioch, puts it just about right.

> Just as a man must keep a mirror polished, so he must keep his soul pure. When there is rust on a mirror, a man's face cannot be seen in it; so also when there is sin in a man, such a man cannot see God.
>
> But if you will you can be cured. Deliver yourself to the physician, and he will cure the eyes of your soul and heart. Who is the physician? He is God, who heals and gives life through the Word and Wisdom... If you know these things, and live in purity, holiness, and righteousness, you can see God. (Theophilus of Antioch, addressed to Autolycus, Breviary, Lent Week 3 Office of Readings, Wednesday, p. 158, vol. II, London, Collins, 1972.)

If a person is pure in heart, you can trust his or her motives. That person's motives will not be corrupt. Chastity is not running away from real life, an opting out. It can and is intended to lead to real love, which is not the same as feelings. It is truly willing the other person's good, and not wishing pleasure from that person:

> 2346 Charity is the *form* of all the virtues. Under its influence, chastity appears as a school of the gift of the person. Self-mastery is ordered to the gift of self. Chastity leads him who practises it to become a witness to his neighbour of God's fidelity and loving kindness.

> 2347 The virtue of chastity blossoms in friendship. It shows the disciple how to follow and imitate him who has chosen us as his friends, who has given himself totally to us and allows us to participate in his divine estate. Chastity is a promise of immortality.
>
> Chastity is expressed notably in *friendship with one's neighbour*. Whether it develops between persons of the same or opposite sex, friendship represents a great good for all. It leads to spiritual communion.

Chastity is a supreme example of humanisation. We become human when the natural instincts are purified and transformed. Thus everyone admires great courage, when a person performs superhuman feats by climbing Everest or sailing around the world in a small boat. The virtue of chastity enables human beings to love God and other people with a pure heart, and so opens the eyes to their goodness in friendship.

We have a decision to make, for or against chastity:

> 2339 Chastity includes an apprenticeship in self-mastery which is a training in human freedom. The alternative is clear: either man governs his passions and finds peace, or he lets himself be dominated by them and becomes unhappy.

Q. Does not that put married people, who are presumably unchaste, at a disadvantage here?

A. The Catholic Church has spoken much in recent years about 'married chastity', not in the sense of a married couple abstaining from sexual union, but rather seeing the married union of body and soul, fully expressed in the act of intercourse:

> 2337 Chastity means the successful integration of sexuality within the person and thus the inner unity of man in his bodily and spiritual being. Sexuality, in which man's belonging to the bodily and biological world is expressed, becomes personal and truly human when it is integrated into the relationship of one person to another, in the complete and lifelong mutual gift of a man and a woman.

Chastity, therefore, can be fulfilled in marriage because, in sexual intercourse, man and woman become completely themselves, body and spirit fully united, giving themselves to each other in physical/spiritual union. In this case, their sexual organs are being used in the right way: enjoying sex in the right way, but also exercising due moderation with respect to each other and their genuine needs.

Most commendable in scripture is the moderation of Tobias, in the Old Testament, quoted in the Catechism, who is fearful of a demon destroying him and his newly wed Sarah. Instead of immediately making love to his bride.

> 2361 Tobias got out of bed and said to Sarah, 'Sister, get up, and let us pray and implore our Lord that he grant us mercy and safety.' So she got up, and they began to pray and implore that they might be kept safe. Tobias began by saying, 'Blessed are you, O God of our fathers... You made Adam, and for him you made

his wife Eve as a helper and support. From the two of them the race of mankind has sprung. You said, "It is not good that the man should be alone; let us make a helper for him like himself." I now am taking this kinswoman of mine, not because of lust, but with sincerity. Grant that she and I may find mercy and that we may grow old together.' And they both said, 'Amen, Amen.' Then they went to sleep for the night.

Tobit 8:4-9

Tobias and Sarah were practising married chastity. Their making love at the right time, later, would be all the more pleasurable to them, because they had put God first before their passion for each other. They would be rewarded by true love, both of body and of spirit.

For the Catechism, therefore, each person is called to a life of chastity, but each in their own way:

> 2349 'People should cultivate [chastity] in the way that is suited to their state of life. Some profess virginity or consecrated celibacy which enables them to give themselves to God alone with an undivided heart in a remarkable manner. Others live in the way prescribed for all by the moral law, whether they are married or single.' Married people are called to live conjugal chastity; others practise chastity in continence.

As early as the sixth century, Bishop Ambrose of Milan could give a most balanced view of the variety of the roads to chastity: There are three forms of the virtue of chastity: the first is that of spouses, the second that of widows and the third that of virgins. We do not praise any one of them to the exclusion of the others... This is what makes for the richness of the discipline of the Church. (Quoted in *CCC* 2349 from Ambrose, *De Viduis* 4.23.)

One married man said to me once, after many years of happy marriage, 'Sex is important, but not half as important as some people make it out to be. And, as time goes on, it becomes less important.' The relationship of that man and woman had deepened into the gift of friendship, the fruit of true charity with each other, in its most intimate form, marriage. Any marriage which develops into that kind of special friendship is truly a chaste marriage.

For the unmarried person, also, chastity can be the basis of the deepest friendships between different sexes, and between members of the same sex. Speaking as a celibate priest, I have found friendship with women one of the greatest strengths of my priesthood. Chastity should not lead to cold-fish, sexless individuals, but those whose sexuality has been integrated into love of God and of people.

Q. If you are right, also, it would seem that large numbers of people will never have any sex at all. Not only priests, monks and nuns, but widows and widowers, single parents without a partner, people with solely homosexual tendencies. Are not they really missing something, to have to go without sex? Is chastity for them even possible or desirable?

A. It is worth remembering that large numbers of people go without sex daily. We do not expect children, of whom there are millions, to have sex for the first fifteen years of their life, although the general promiscuity today is encouraging them to have sex earlier and earlier. Many old people, of whom there are increasing numbers today, can live perfectly happy lives without sex. My mother and aunt were both widowed early in their married lives. They lived together as sisters for fifty years, quite happily, without sex. Many people will put off marriage in order to look after a parent or brother or sister. These people often become very unselfish in character, and use their celibacy to grow as persons, rather than as a deprivation.

It is often thought that the Old Testament discourages

celibacy and encourages marriage. But that is not entirely true. Centuries at least before Christ, a prophetic writer encouraged those who could not have children:

> For thus says the Lord: To the eunuchs who keep my Sabbaths, who choose the things that please me and hold fast my covenant, I will give, in my house and within my walls, a monument and a name better than sons and daughters; I will give them an everlasting name that shall not be cut off.
>
> Is 56:4-5

With younger adults, and of course some older people too, chastity is very difficult. But it is quite wrong to think that it is impossible, even though, as we shall see in a moment, to conquer passion may take years. If our analysis of human nature is correct, then our sexual organs are ordered towards procreation and so marital communion by God. In making us this way, therefore, it would follow that we should be able freely to limit our sexual activity within the laws of God, that is within marriage.

The problem is, of course, the old enemy Original Sin. The Church teaches that, by our baptism, we as Christians are set free from the sin of our first parents by the infusion of the grace of the presence of God the Holy Spirit. We are cleansed of sin. However, the effects of Original Sin, like a scar, remain in what is called by theologians 'concupiscence', i.e. disordered desire:

> 1264 Yet certain temporal consequences of sin remain in the baptised, such as suffering, illness, death, and such frailties inherent in life as weaknesses of character, and so on, as well as an inclination to sin that Tradition calls concupiscence, or metaphorically, 'the tinder for sin' (*fomes peccati*); since concupiscence, 'is left for us to wrestle with. It cannot harm those who do not consent but manfully resist it by the grace of Jesus

93

Christ'. Indeed, 'an athlete is not crowned unless he competes according to the rules.'

Christians will always have a struggle on their hands. But, with the help of the Holy Spirit, the message is that they can win.

Q. But this all sounds rather idealistic. What happens when it all goes wrong?

A. Now we get down, as they say, to the nitty-gritty!

10

Sin, forgiveness and responsibility

Q. Why does the Catholic Church consider that some sexual acts are sins?

A. Let us first of all think of what constitutes a sin. The Catechism states:

> 1849 Sin is an offence against reason, truth and right conscience; it is failure in genuine love for God and neighbour caused by a perverse attachment to certain goods. It wounds the nature of man and injures human solidarity. It has been defined as 'an utterance, a deed or a desire contrary to the eternal law'.

'Sin' is not a very popular word these days, even among Christians. But it is very clear in the Bible and in the Tradition of the Church. The Gospel (Anglo-Saxon for 'Good News') is bad news before it is good news. The bad news is that we have sinned before God as a human race and as individuals. The good news is that Jesus Christ came to earth to suffer and to die for us to forgive us our sins. By baptism, the Christian is saved, redeemed by the blood of Christ, with all his or her sins forgiven. There is a completely new start.

But baptism is only the beginning of new life. There is

a journey to go, through the 'wilderness' of this world to the Promised Land of heaven. And, as St Paul tells those wayward Corinthians, there is no guaranteed ticket home without our own co-operation:

I do not want you to be unaware, brothers and sisters, that our ancestors were all under the cloud, and all passed through the sea, and all were baptised into Moses in the cloud and in the sea, and all ate the same spiritual food, and all drank the same spiritual drink. For they drank from the spiritual rock that followed them, and the rock was Christ. Nevertheless, God was not pleased with most of them, and they were struck down in the wilderness. Now these things occurred as examples for us, so that we might not desire evil as they did. Do not become idolaters as some of them did; as it is written, 'The people sat down to eat and drink, and they rose up to play.' We must not indulge in sexual immorality as some of them did, and twenty-three thousand fell in a single day. We must not put Christ to the test, as some of them did, and were destroyed by serpents. And do not complain as some of them did, and were destroyed by the destroyer.

These things happened to them to serve as an example, and they were written down to instruct us, on whom the ends of the ages have come. So if you think you are standing, watch out that you do not fall. No testing has overtaken you that is not common to everyone. God is faithful, and he will not let you be tested beyond your strength, but with the testing he will also provide the way out so that you may be able to endure it.

1 Corinthians 10:1-13

The bad news is that we can fall into sin. The good news is that we can always be forgiven and start a new life again. 'If we say that we have no sin, we deceive ourselves, and the truth is not in us. If we confess our sins, he who is faithful and just will forgive us our sins and cleanse us from all unrighteousness' (1 Jn 1:8-9).

Q. I understand that the (Catholic Church teaches that some sexual sins such as adultery are 'mortal sins'. What can that mean?

A. Firstly, the Church divides sin into 'mortal' and 'venial':

> 1854 Sins are rightly evaluated according to their gravity. The distinction between mortal and venial sin, already evident in Scripture, became part of the tradition of the Church. It is corroborated by human experience.

> 1855 *Mortal sin* destroys charity in the heart of man by a grave violation of God's law; it turns man away from God, who is his ultimate end and his beatitude, by preferring an inferior good to him.
> *Venial sin* allows charity to subsist, even though it offends and wounds it.

A mortal sin, i.e. a 'deadly' sin, is called so because it is an act of disobedience which destroys the love of God in us. St Paul gives examples of sins which make us unworthy of the Kingdom of Heaven. That means that the love of God is destroyed in us, and we are excluded by our own actions from communion with the Church: 'Now the works of the flesh are obvious: fornication, impurity, licentiousness, idolatry, sorcery, enmities, strife, jealousy, anger, quarrels, dissensions, factions, envy, drunkenness, carousing, and things like these. I am warning you, as I warned you before: those who do such things will not inherit the Kingdom of God' (Gal 5:19-21).

Incidentally, by 'flesh' here (Greek *sarx)* Paul means our disordered nature as a result of Original Sin. He does not mean that the body itself is evil, only that sin entering in has disordered the seat of our desires, where sin has its

97

Kingdom. From this *sarx* come all our evil thoughts and deeds.

The Catechism tells us that mortal sin, in destroying the love of God in our souls, needs radical repentance to restore our damaged relationship with God the source of our final happiness:

> 1856 Mortal sin, by attacking the vital principle within us – that is, charity – necessitates a new initiative of God's mercy and a conversion of heart which is normally accomplished within the setting of the sacrament of reconciliation:
>
>> When the will sets itself upon something that is of its nature incompatible with the charity that orients man toward his ultimate end, then the sin is mortal by its very object... whether it contradicts the love of God, such as blasphemy or perjury, or the love of neighbour, such as homicide or adultery... But when the sinner's will is set upon something that of its nature involves a disorder, but is not opposed to the love of God and neighbour, such as thoughtless chatter or immoderate laughter and the like, such sins are venial.
>
>> St Thomas Aquinas
>> *Summa Theologiae*, I-II, 88, 2, corp. art.

Q. If a sin is mortal, and a person dies in a state of mortal sin, according to the Catholic Church they will go to hell, the place of separation from God. Surely God could not do this, if he is a loving God?

A. God is infinite love. He never ceases to love us, as our Creator, whatever we do. But he respects our freedom, even to reject his love. And he cannot accept evil when it is serious and deliberate against his laws, written in the Scriptures, and in our hearts as humans. Our relationship with

God is subject to damage, even fatal damage, due to our own fault.

We know that this is the case in marriage. Even in today's free-sex society, it is accepted that a married couple may separate if one (say the husband) has been unfaithful. Their married love has been damaged by his act of infidelity. The wife may even say, 'I still love him. I will never stop loving him. But I cannot live with him any more, I cannot share his life, his bed, after what he has done.'

Love can be destroyed. The message of the Scriptures is that our relationship with God can be destroyed if we are unfaithful in loving God or our neighbour. By marriage, the couple owe each other love, just as a child owes love to its parents. When that love is given to someone else, the relationship with God is harmed seriously. That wife says to her husband, 'How can you really love me if you have spent the night with her?' The husband may protest that it meant nothing, that one night stand. But, in reality, they both know that their love bond has been broken by that act of infidelity. The whole marriage, the whole family, is in danger of being split up.

The prophet Ezekiel uses explicitly sexual language to describe how our relationship with God can be destroyed through infidelity. He is addressing Israel as a community. But his words apply also to individuals, who can 'play the harlot' with God:

Thus you longed for the lewdness of your youth, when the Egyptians fondled your bosom and caressed your young breasts. Therefore, O Oholibah, thus says the Lord God: I will rouse against you your lovers from whom you turned in disgust, and I will bring them against you from every side: the Babylonians and all the Chaldeans, Pekod and Shoa and Koa, and all the Assyrians with them, handsome young men, governors and commanders all of them, officers and warriors, all of them riding on horses. They shall come against you from the north with chariots and wagons and a host of peoples; they shall set themselves against you on every side with buckler, shield, and helmet, and I will commit the judgement to them, and they shall judge you according to their ordinances. I will direct my indignation against you, in order that they may deal with you in fury. They shall cut off your nose and your ears, and your survivors shall fall by the sword. They shall seize your sons and your daughters, and your survivors shall be devoured by fire. They shall also strip you of your clothes and take away your fine jewels. So I will put an end to your lewdness and your whoring brought from the land of Egypt; you shall not long for them, or remember Egypt any more.

Ezekiel 23:21-27

Ezekiel is here making a comparison between adultery and idolatry. In fact, the two were often linked. Some of the pagan rites of those times included not only the sacrificing of firstborn children, but also acts of lewd sexuality as ritual. The prophet is accusing his people of bringing those pagan ideas from Egypt and corrupting the Kingdom. As a result Oholibah (Ezekiel's nickname for Judah, the King-dom centred in Jerusalem, the City of David) would be ravaged by the rapacious hoards of Babylon.

Ezekiel spent most of his life as an exile in Babylon, away from the Promised Land, in the sixth century BC. He lived through the rape of Jerusalem by the Babylonians in 596 and 587, when the Temple was destroyed, and the king taken captive. It seemed that all the promises God made to David had been lost by the sin of the people.

But Ezekiel helped the people there in a foreign land to bring good out of that situation. He promised that they would return to their land, with the cleansing of the Holy Spirit. God's mercy was greater than their infidelity. But, Ezekiel insisted, they did not have to wait until then to serve God. They could individually come to God by true repentance for sin. They could change their lives, and 'live', not spiritually 'die'. Even if a father was guilty of sin, his son could follow another way:

> But if this man has a son who sees all the sins that his father has done, considers, and does not do likewise, who does not eat upon the mountains or lift up his eyes to the idols of the house of Israel, does not defile his neighbour's wife, does not wrong anyone, exacts no pledge, commits no robbery, but gives his bread to the hungry and covers the naked with a garment, withholds his hand from iniquity, takes no advance or accrued interest, observes my ordinances, and follows my statutes; he shall not die for his father's iniquity; he shall surely live. As for his father, because he practised extortion, robbed his brother, and did what is not good among his people, he dies for his iniquity.
>
> Ezekiel 18:14-18

The Scriptures tell us that change is always possible. It is up to each one as an individual, whether we 'live' or 'die', that is whether we follow God's path of love and fidelity, or the way of sin that leads to spiritual death, the loss of the love of God in us.

Q. But does the Church teach that every sexual sin is a mortal sin?

A. The Church teaches that deliberate acts against the Sixth and Ninth Commandment, when the person committing those acts is fully aware, fully free and knows of their gravity, are mortal sins. This would include acts of adultery, fornication, contraception, homosexual acts, masturbation, paedophilia, bestiality, and sadomasochism; also deliberate thoughts desiring to perform those acts, when that desire is fully consented to in the mind and in the heart.

Cf the words of Jesus (Mt 5:27-8) quoted above. As we have seen, the Church in its living Tradition extends the meaning of 'You shall not commit adultery' to include any kind of sexual immorality.

All these acts involve a decision against the love of neighbour, using the members of our body, our sexual organs, not for the purpose for which they were ordained by God – to create and foster love open to life within marriage – but to pursue a pleasure misusing those sexual organs.

But, having said this, we must immediately add that not every act which is objectively a serious act against the sixth commandment is performed with full knowledge and consent. The Catechism makes this perfectly clear:

1859 Mortal sin requires *full knowledge and complete consent.* It presupposes knowledge of the sinful character of the act, of its opposition to God's law. It also implies a consent sufficiently deliberate to be a personal choice. Feigned ignorance and hardness of heart do not diminish, but rather increase, the voluntary character of a sin.

1860 *Unintentional ignorance* can diminish or even remove the imputability of a grave offence. But no one is deemed to be ignorant of the principles of the moral law, which are written in the conscience of every man. The prompting of feelings and passions can also diminish the voluntary and free character of the offence, as can external pressures or pathological disorders. Sin committed through malice, by deliberate choice of evil, is the gravest.

Read the above words very carefully if you think you have committed a mortal sin, particularly in the sexual sphere, where passion is so likely to take away at least partially such full deliberation and consent. Always ask yourself, was it deliberate, and was there full consent on my part?

To give some examples. All these examples are of diminished responsibility, or at least of possibly diminished responsibility:

- A nocturnal emission while asleep (a 'wet dream'). That is not even a sin, because it is not voluntary. It is a purely motor activity of the body, without our mind or will involved.
- A mother who is pressured by her husband to have contraceptive sex; for economic reasons they can have no more children. All attempts to persuade her husband to try NFP are to no avail.
- A young person sorely tempted to masturbate. He is seriously trying to overcome the habit, but he gives in sometimes, especially after seeing a sexy film on TV.
- A young person who is deceived into going to a gay party, and is seduced into homosexual sex.

On the other hand, a person may have to ask: did I really know, in accepting a dinner date, that they would ask me round to 'my place'? Did I really go to that dinner date because, deep down, I wanted to go round to their place? In such a case, a true act of the will was involved against the sin. Self-deceit is very common in matters regarding sexual temptation. That is why the confessional is so important in these matters.

Q. What does a Catholic do when he or she has committed a mortal sin?

A. The rule of the Catholic Church's Canon Law is that a Catholic must confess mortal sins at least once per year, during the Easter period. However, a Catholic with a serious or mortal sin on their conscience should really go to confession as soon as reasonably possible, within a week or so. A general rule which I have followed as a confessor is to advise people to confess anything which is objectively a mortal sin (adultery, fornication, masturbation, etc.), even if it is probably committed without full deliberation and consent. This will have the effect of giving peace to that person's conscience, and will help to strengthen that person against future temptation.

People will find that the priest is most gentle, especially regarding sexual sins. The priest is aware of the weakness of human nature. He is human too! He is in this way like the priests of the Old Testament, but representing Christ the High Priest. 'He is able to deal gently with the ignorant and wayward, since he himself is subject to weakness' (Heb 5:2).

It is important to remember that all sins can be forgiven by God, provided that we are sorry, and determined to try to live a life in accordance with God's law. Christ our Lord and the Church are really happy when someone asks forgiveness, and returns to follow Christ. Remember the parable told by Jesus himself:

> Which one of you, having a hundred sheep and losing one of them, does not leave the ninety-nine in the wilderness and go after the one that is lost until he finds it? When he has found it, he lays it on his shoulders and rejoices. And when he comes home, he calls together his friends and neighbours, saying to them, 'Rejoice with me, for I have found my sheep that was lost.' Just so, I tell you, there will be more joy in heaven over one sinner who repents than over ninety-nine righteous persons who need no repentance.
>
> Luke 15:4-7

So, if you think you have committed a mortal sin:

- Make an act of sorrow or penance immediately, e.g. say Psalm 51, 'Have mercy upon me, O God ...', or an Act of Contrition.
- Go to confession as soon as is reasonably possible.

- Promise to avoid the occasions of sin in the future.
- Do not be discouraged! Thank God that he has given you the grace to confess your sins and promise to do better in the future.
- Receive Holy Communion as soon as possible afterwards in thanksgiving.

Remember, canonised saints have been guilty of sexual sins. Margaret of Cortona, for instance, fell in love with a young courtier, and gave him a child. She repented, and spent her life running hospitals and nursing the poor. She is now *St* Margaret of Cortona! Could I commend her as the patron saint of all those who have committed sexual sins?

11

Why marry?

Q. Increasingly here in Western society, marriage is becoming less and less frequent. Young people are deciding to live together without the full commitment of marriage. Is that much less hypocritical than marrying 'for life', and then splitting up after a couple of years, as so many marriages do today?

A. The Catechism is clear in condemning this practice as against the law of God, and gives the reasons:

> 2390 In a so-called *free union*, a man and a woman refuse to give juridical and public form to a liaison involving sexual intimacy.
>
> The expression 'free union' is fallacious: what can 'union' mean when the partners make no commitment to one another, each exhibiting a lack of trust in the other, in himself, or in the future?
>
> The expression covers a number of different situations: concubinage, rejection of marriage as such, or inability to make long-term commitments. All these situations offend against the dignity of marriage; they destroy the very idea of the family; they weaken the sense of fidelity. They are contrary to the moral law.

The sexual act must take place exclusively within marriage. Outside of marriage it always constitutes a grave sin and excludes one from sacramental communion.

This mentality against marriage was dramatically presented in the harsh cynicism of the phenomenally successful *Four Weddings and a Funeral* in the late eighties. In this British Oscar-winning film, a young man (Hugh Grant) goes to a succession of weddings to which he has been invited by his friends. He himself is living with a partner he has not yet married. The wedding ceremonies are generally presented as a sham, covering up all kinds of relationships which are extra-marital. The clergyman (comedian Rowan Atkinson) performing the ceremony is a hopeless figure of fun.

The only point of deep sincerity is the funeral of his homosexual friend, where a poem of W.H. Auden (himself a homosexual) is read out. The two gays are presented as genuinely loving each other, and genuinely faithful to each other. *Four Weddings and a Funeral* ends with Hugh Grant stating to his girl friend that he is not going to marry her, a kind of anti-proposal of marriage.

It is hard to imagine a fiercer attack on the institution of marriage, all brilliantly presented as rollicking comedy. *Four Weddings and a Funeral* is a kind of graphic summary of the philosophy of the newly 'liberated age.

Demographically, this new attitude is having a devastating effect on the numbers marrying at the turn of the millennium. Recently (1999) the British Government Actuaries Department made the following calculations based on present trends:

- Fifty-five percent of the population of England and Wales is now married.
- That number will fall to 48 percent in 2011.
- Those who marry will represent only 45 percent by the year 2021.
- One third of women will never have married by 2011.

- The figure for men who have never married will be 41 percent.
- Some three million couples will live together unmarried by the year 2021.

Birmingham Evening Mail,
Wednesday 27 January 1999, p. 7

The hero (or anti-hero) in *Four Weddings and a Funeral* was certainly convinced that it was more honest not to marry than to go through what appeared to be the empty ritual of getting married, when this meant nothing in terms of permanence and fidelity.

He has a point. Many couples are opting for a 'relationship' which is open-ended, with marriage as an option after a number of years living together, rather than immediately embarking on the full commitment of marriage. The reason why marriage is often so unpopular an institution today is that so many marriages in fact fail; but this is largely because we are living in an age where sex is for pleasure in itself, and has little or nothing to do with fidelity and only a loose relationship with procreation. Secular society, business interest, is geared to stimulate the erotic sexuality of the human being in every aspect of life.

Put simply, even naively, the difference between this age and former ages is this: that before, even though the pleasure of sex was never considered unimportant, sex was mainly seen as related to having a family. In this day and age, since the recent 'sexual revolution', sex is mainly seen as a pleasurable activity, like eating or playing sport. Any attempt to restrict it (apart from paedophilia and possibly sadomasochistic activity and bestiality) must be considered to be prudish and old fashioned. The only wrong sex is what is called 'unsafe sex', that is sex where a sexually transmitted disease may result; or 'irresponsible sex', which is sex which may result in an unwanted child. This links up the sexual revolution in a major way with the whole development of the contraceptive society.

As we have argued throughout, if the link between sex and procreation within the permanent relationship of marriage is broken, the sexual anarchy which is the situation today becomes the inevitable consequence. It is just straight logic. Even many Catholics were deceived when *Humanae Vitae* was first issued. They thought that it was just a case of good Catholic parents being able to use the pill within a stable marriage situation. They did not realise that, by accepting the contraceptive principle within marriage, they were undermining the whole rationale of Catholic sexual ethics.

The twin pillars of the Catholic doctrine of sexuality, based as we have seen upon Natural Law, ordained by the Creator, are:

- **The procreative aspect**: That the sexual organs are given to us by God for the procreation of new life. Thus any act which actively excludes this procreative function happening is gravely wrong, and against God's law..
- **The unitive aspect**: That the sexual organs are male–female orientated. This is order that the pleasure of male-female sexual union will aid the bonding of a permanent relationship between the man and the woman. Thus the offspring of this union, new human beings each with an immortal soul, will enjoy the stability of this permanent relationship in order to grow and themselves learn to love God and neighbour.

The teaching of the Catholic Church on marriage reaches its climax in its belief in the unity and indissolubility of marriage. The sacramental dimension of marriage, where marriage becomes a means of God's grace to the couple, brings together all aspects of the marriage relationship to become a spiritual union, a sign of the mystical relationship between Christ and his Church (Eph 5:32):

1644   The love of the spouses requires, of its very nature, the unity and indissolubility of the spouses' community of persons, which embraces their entire life: 'so they are no longer two, but one flesh'. They are 'called to grow continually in their communion through day-to-day fidelity to their marriage promise of total mutual self-giving.' This human communion is confirmed, purified and completed by communion in Jesus Christ, given through the Sacrament of Matrimony. It is deepened by lives of the common faith and by the Eucharist received together.

1645   The unity of marriage, distinctly recognised by our Lord, is made clear in the equal personal dignity which must be accorded to man and wife in mutual and unreserved affection.' *Polygamy* is contrary to conjugal love which is undivided and exclusive.

1646   By its very nature conjugal love requires the inviolable fidelity of the spouses. This is the consequence of the gift of themselves which they make to each other. Love seeks to be definitive; it cannot be an arrangement 'until further notice'. The 'intimate union of marriage, as a mutual giving of two persons, and the good of the children, demand total fidelity from the spouses and require an unbreakable union between them.'

Governments are beginning to see the benefits of the right view of marriage as presented by the Church's Tradition; and I mean here all Christian churches, Catholic, Orthodox, Anglican or Protestant. The cost to the country of broken marriages is enormous. Billions of pounds must be handed out to single parents in aid. The psychological damage is also incalculable to the children of broken and of less than permanent unions. What is even more incalculable is the harm done to human relationships in terms of angry quarrels and the tensions of insecurity within the family. This insecurity is rooted precisely in the separation of the sexual act from any necessary link with procreation, and is separated consequently from the lifelong faithful union between the married couple. No one is able to give any sound ethical answer to the question, 'Why shouldn't I have a little bit on the side?' Why not, indeed, if sex is purely for pleasure? There is therefore a desperate need to return to the tradition of married fidelity, rooted in the Christian theology of sexuality.

Of course there is hypocrisy in a marriage ceremony if the whole of society does not really expect marriage to be permanent; and that lack of expectation is shared by the couple themselves. But it would in no way be hypocrisy if the couple decided, after a suitable period of engagement, to consecrate their lives to each other totally, for life, and to accept as a gift of God any children given to them by God. Even if the marriage subsequently failed, it at least began right. And, having begun right, surely there must be a much better chance of success.

Q. OK, I will grant you this point, that we need to return to a more traditional pattern of marriage. But you would surely concede this, that it is better for young people today to live together for a while, to see if it will work, rather than embarking on lifelong union without really knowing each other.

A. The *Catechism of the Catholic Church* is equally discouraging about the whole idea of trial marriages:

> 2391 Some today claim a 'right to a trial marriage' where there is an intention of getting married later. However firm the purpose of those who engage in premature sexual relations may be, 'the fact is that such liaisons can scarcely ensure mutual sincerity and fidelity in a relationship between a man and a woman, nor,

especially, can they protect it from inconstancy of desires or whim.' Carnal union is morally legitimate only when a definitive community of life between a man and woman has been established. Human love does not tolerate 'trial marriages'. It demands a total and definitive gift of persons to one another.

A 'trial marriage' must be wrong objectively because, during the trial period, the couple are having sex together outside of the permanent commitment of marriage. For a couple to get to know each other well is important. That is why the Catholic Church is more and more insisting upon a period of instruction of six months or more for engaged couples. That means that the role of the engagement is more and more seen as vital to ensure a well-prepared couple:

> 2350 Those who are *engaged to marry* are called to live chastity in continence. They should see in this time of testing a discovery of mutual respect, an apprenticeship in fidelity and the hope of receiving one another from God. They should reserve for marriage the expressions of affection that belong to married love. They will help each other grow in chastity.

The engagement period is first and foremost for the couple to learn to love each other, to begin to learn each other's strengths and weaknesses; and to get to know each other without sex. The whole of Christian tradition says that this is a better preparation for marriage than having sex together. This tradition has worked for two thousand years. This is most of all because it develops trust between the couple. If both abstain from sex during this period, then they are much more likely to trust each other, and to remain trustworthy after marriage, when inevitable temptations will occur, especially in the sexual climate today.

There are rare instances where the couple find that they

are unable to have sex together. Those who advise trial marriages use this small number of cases as an argument for a period of sexual probation. But there are many solutions to this problem without advocating fornication prior to marriage. The Church allows separation and remarriage where a marriage has not been consummated, because it considers the act of sexual intercourse as a part of the marriage union, together with the exchange of vows between the couple. In an extreme instance, therefore, the newly married couple could separate and remarry. (A Catholic couple would have to prove non-consummation in a church court.)

Otherwise, the couple could see both a doctor and a marriage counsellor to discover what the problem is, and how it could be resolved. Other couples find that adoption is the answer. They live quite happily together without sex, and find the fruitfulness of their marriage in taking in a child who was perhaps abandoned. Unfortunately, the number of children available for adoption has decreased dramatically, largely owing to the wide prevalence of abortion.

Nothing, of course, prevents a couple from seeing a doctor and/or a counsellor before marriage. Sexual problems could well be identified without pre-marital sex, just by an examination. St Thomas More, the Chancellor of England (i.e. the Prime Minister) during the reign of Henry VIII, who was beheaded for his loyalty to the Pope, refusing to acknowledge the king as head of the Church, wrote a book called *Utopia,* in which he depicted what he considered to be the ideal society. I suspect that much of the time, in writing this book, his tongue was in his cheek. He advocated that married couples should see each other in the nude before they married, each of course accompanied by a suitable chaperon during the disrobing! This was on the principle that you did not commit yourself to a product until you had inspected it unwrapped. Seriously, when in doubt, a medical check-up is a good idea.

In any case, the Church rejects any process of bringing a child to birth which does not involve sexual union between the couple. That is on the second principle, that the sex act to be morally right must be an act of physical union between the spouses, in order to foster their love together and that of the child. That is why the practice of *in vitro fertilisation* is morally unacceptable to the Church. The child is born in this case, not from a union between the spouses, but by a mechanical process. Again, therefore, this is against the natural law in the sense of the two-in-one-flesh of Genesis:

2376 Techniques that entail the dissociation of husband and wife, by the intrusion of a person other than the couple (donation of sperm or ovum, surrogate uterus), are gravely immoral. These techniques (heterologous artificial insemination and fertilisation) infringe the child's right to be born of a father and mother known to him and bound to each other by marriage. They betray the spouses' 'right to become a father and a mother only through each other'.

2377 Techniques involving only the married couple (homologous artificial insemination and fertilisation) are perhaps less reprehensible, yet remain morally unacceptable. They dissociate the sexual act from the procreative act. The act which brings the child into existence is no longer an act by which two persons give themselves to one another, but one that 'entrusts the life and identity of the embryo into the power of doctors and biologists and establishes the domination of technology over the origin and destiny of the human person. Such a relationship of domination is in itself contrary to the dignity and equality that must be common to parents and children.' 'Under the moral aspect procreation is deprived of its proper perfection when it is not willed as the fruit of the conjugal act, that is to say, of the specific act of the spouses' union... Only respect for the link between the meanings of the conjugal act and respect for the unity of the human being make possible procreation in conformity with the dignity of the person.'

2378 A child is not something *owed* to one, but is a *gift*. The 'supreme gift of marriage' is a human person. A child may not be considered a piece of property, an idea to which an alleged 'right to a child' would lead. In this area, only the child possesses genuine rights: the right 'to be the fruit of the specific act of the conjugal love of his parents', and 'the right to be respected as a person from the moment of his conception'.

2379 The Gospel shows that physical sterility is not an absolute evil. Spouses who still suffer from infertility after exhausting legitimate medical procedures should unite themselves with the Lord's Cross, the source of all spiritual fecundity. They can give expression to their generosity by adopting abandoned children or performing demanding services for others.

Q. But how is it possible to make that kind of commitment for life? What happens when the man or the woman falls in love with someone else?

A. The *Catechism of the Catholic Church* tells us how:

2364 The married couple forms 'the intimate partnership of life and love established by the Creator and governed by his laws; it is rooted in the conjugal covenant, that is, in their irrevocable personal consent.' Both give themselves definitively and totally to one another. They are no longer two; from now on they form one flesh. The covenant they freely contracted imposes on the spouses the obligation to preserve it as unique and indissoluble. 'What therefore God has joined together, let not man put asunder.'

2365 Fidelity expresses constancy in keeping one's given word. God is faithful. The Sacrament of Matrimony enables man and woman to enter into Christ's fidelity for his Church. Through conjugal chastity, they bear witness to this mystery before the world.

> St John Chrysostom suggests that young husbands should say to their wives: I have taken you in my arms, and I love you, and I prefer you to my life itself. For the present life is nothing, and my most ardent dream is to spend it with you in such a way that we may be assured of not being separated in the life reserved for us... I place your love above all things, and nothing would be more bitter or painful to me than to be of a different mind than you.
>
> St John Chrysostom,
> *Homiliae in ad Ephesios*, 20, 8: PG62, 146-7

Millions of couples down the centuries have lived this way, sharing their ups and downs, their problems with each other. And the act of conjugal union has been an essential part of their happiness, their joy in each other's bodies. Why change a Christian ethic which has stood the test of time because of a consumerist, hedonistic philosophy of non-marriage, boosted by big business and the media?

Q. This sounds all very well, idealistic. But what happens when the ideal is not realised?

A. Again, the Church has been used to dealing with imperfect human beings, and consequently imperfect marriages. Particularly in this day and age, we could see the situation arising where couples who are living together casually want to make their relationship permanent in the bond of marriage. They might even be convinced by the arguments for God's law presented in this book!

In all these situations, it is necessary for couples to discuss matters with their local priest, and if possible also with a marriage counsellor. Marriage is not necessarily the answer; although the Church cannot morally permit sex to continue between the couple if they remain unmarried. But, with a will and with a commitment to follow Christ, a solution can and will be found. But never be ashamed to ask for help from the Church, either from a priest or from a marriage counsellor.

12

Divorce and remarriage

Q. Another major problem is the Catholic Church's refusal to allow divorced people to remarry while the previous partner is still alive. Is this not totally unrealistic and insensitive in this day and age?

A. This aspect of Roman Catholic teaching goes back to Jesus' own teaching regarding marriage and divorce. We will have to repeat what we have already said regarding scriptural arguments. They are hardly ever watertight. But what we can say in this instance is that there are good scriptural grounds, grounds in the teaching of Jesus himself, for the Catholic teaching that a valid marriage between two baptised Christians cannot be torn asunder' (cf Matthew 19:6) while the partners are still living, so that a subsequent marriage of either of the partners will be invalid. The Church adds its authority, and the authority of Tradition, to what is a sound scriptural argument.

This again seems to be very tough and uncompromising, particularly in the modern situation where divorce and remarriage are so frequent. This is even more difficult granted that now in the majority of Western countries, including those with a majority of Catholics, divorce and remarriage are possible in law. But the new Catechism does not give way an inch:

1650   Today there are numerous Catholics in many
countries who have recourse to civil *divorce* and contract
new civil unions. In fidelity to the words of Jesus Christ
'Whoever divorces his wife and marries another,
commits adultery against her; and if she divorces her
husband and marries another, she commits adultery' –
the Church maintains that a new union cannot be
recognised as valid, if the first marriage was. If the
divorced are remarried civilly, they find themselves
in a situation that objectively contravenes God's
law. Consequently, they cannot receive Eucharistic
communion as long as this situation persists.

This teaching was clearly stated in the Council of Trent:

If anyone says the church erroneously taught and
teaches, according to evangelical and apostolic doctrine,
that the bond of marriage cannot be dissolved by the
adultery of one of the spouses, and that neither party,
even the innocent one who gave no grounds for the
adultery, can contract another marriage while their
spouse is still living; and that the husband commits
adultery who dismisses an adulterous wife and takes
another woman, as does the wife dismissing an
adulterous husband and marrying another man; let him
be anathema. (Tanner, II, Trent, Session 24, Canons on
the Sacrament of Marriage, No. 7 p. 754, lines 40 to
755, line 4.)

The key text here is Matthew 19:3-9, which we now quote
in full:

Some Pharisees came to him, and to test him they
asked, 'Is it lawful for a man to divorce his wife for any
cause?' He answered 'Have you not read that the one
who made them at the beginning 'made them male and
female' and said 'for this reason a man shall leave his

father and mother and be joined to his wife and the two shall become one flesh'? So they are no longer two, but one flesh. Therefore what God has joined together, let no one separate.' They said to him, 'Why then did Moses command us to give a certificate of dismissal and to divorce her?' He said to them, 'It was because you were so hard-hearted that Moses allowed you to divorce your wives, but from the beginning it was not so and I say to you, whoever divorces his wife, except for unchastity and marries another commits adultery.' His disciples said to him, 'If such is the case of a man with his wife, it is better not to marry.'

The background to this discussion is well known. There was a Rabbinic dispute concerning the Mosaic Law in Deuteronomy 24:1, where a man was allowed to divorce his wife (note that the woman was not allowed to divorce her husband!), provided that he gave her a writ of dismissal, which would leave her free to marry another man. The rabbis disputed the grounds giving a man the right to divorce his wife. The rigorist Hillel school demanded that the wife had committed some infidelity in order for the man to have the right to divorce her. The laxist Shammai school, on the other hand, claimed that the man could divorce his wife even for cooking him a bad meal.

The reply of Jesus took everyone by surprise by its strictness. He teaches that there is to be no divorce and remarriage at all. He even reinforces the Genesis text. What God has united, human beings must not divide' with an even stronger statement, 'Now I say this to you: anyone who divorces his wife – I am not speaking of an illicit marriage – and marries another is guilty of adultery'. No wonder the disciples are shocked, and wonder if marriage is worth it at all! (Mt 19:10-12).

The discussion over the meaning of this statement of Jesus about marriage and divorce has been continuous. But it seems to me to reduce itself to three main positions:

- Jesus is not being 'legalistic', only presenting an ideal. But this position is difficult to sustain exegetically. If Jesus was simply saying, 'The ideal is indissoluble union, but I am not being legalistic', then all would agree, but it would have no practical effect. No doubt both the Hillel and the Shammai schools would posit lifelong union as an ideal; but it does not answer their question about what reasons would make divorce and remarriage justifiable. Second, the way in which Jesus expresses the matter leads us to think that he is stating a *conditional law* as in the Old Testament. 'If… then'(cf Leviticus 5). If… then the man is actually committing the crime of adultery in Jewish law.

- Jesus is stating a law, but provides an exception to the law of divorce and remarriage in the famous 'exception clause', 'I am not speaking of an illicit marriage'. If this view was correct, the translation of the exception clause in Greek *mé epi porneia* would be more like 'I am not speaking of marital infidelity'. This is the Eastern Orthodox position, that divorce and remarriage may be allowed for the grounds of infidelity. But there are two great difficulties with this view. The first is that if Jesus meant the exception was for marital infidelity, then the word here used should not be *porneia,* sexual impurity, but *moicheia,* the actual Greek word for 'adultery'. The second is the even more decisive objection that Jesus would be saying nothing at all new in his reply. He would be simply adopting the Hillel position that there had to be serious grounds before divorce and remarriage were allowable. The reply sounds quite radical. The exception clause, in this view, simply takes such radicality from Jesus' reply.

- The third view, expressed in the *New Jerusalem Bible* (*NJB*, Matthew 19:9, note b, p. 1641), is that the exception clause refers to marriages illicit as incestuous since within the forbidden degrees of marriage in Matthew's

Jewish Christian community, as expressed in Leviticus 18. In this case, such marriages would have been considered by Matthew's Christian community as *invalid*, and are not therefore a genuine exception to the rule expressed by Jesus that there is no going back from a valid marriage. This would, of course, support the Roman Catholic rule concerning marriage and divorce. In this case, the exception clause would most likely have been added by the Matthaean community as a clarification of the teaching of Jesus.

Paul most certainly seems to take the same absolute line in 1 Corinthians 7, written, according to the scholars, in 57 AD. He says the following to the Corinthian Christians: 'To the married I give this ruling, and this is not mine but the Lord's; a wife must not be separated from her husband – or, if she has already left him, she must remain unmarried or else be reconciled to her husband – and a husband must not divorce his wife' (1 Cor 7:10-11).

Scholars dispute as to whether the phrase 'and this is not mine but the Lord's refers to a definite body of teaching handed on from Jesus himself forbidding divorce and remarriage (such is not impossible, since the hypothetical document *Q* might well have existed then, or other pre-Gospel collections of Jesus' sayings); or whether and this is not mine but the Lord's' refers rather to a special vision of Paul himself. The former is much more likely in my opinion; but whatever the origin of Paul's teaching on marriage, it appears identical with that which was eventually transmitted as the teaching of Jesus in Matthew.

This surely adds up to a strong argument from the New Testament that the teaching of the Roman Catholic church on the indissolubility of marriage is well based.

We would add here that, in Catholic teaching on marriage, there are three 'goods' (*boni*) of marriage: *fides* (fidelity), *proles* (offspring) and *sacramentum* (sacrament, mystery). Here we focus on the third and spiritual aspect of marriage, that their union is a sacramental sign of the 'union between Christ and his Church' (Eph 5:32). Indeed, even in non-sacramental marriages between non-Christians, we believe that the marriage bond is from God and binds the couple together for life.

This becomes even more important in a Christian marriage, where baptised Christians marry. A sacrament in Catholic theology is a ritual action, ordained by God, as a means of grace. A physical and outward action, e.g. like pouring water in baptism, is elevated by the words 'I baptise you in the name of the Father, and of the Son and of the Holy Spirit' to being the washing of the Holy Spirit cleansing from Original Sin and giving the new life of God to the baptised.

There are seven sacraments ordained by Christ according to the Church: Baptism, Confirmation, Eucharist, Marriage, Ordination, Penance or Reconciliation, and Anointing. All the sacraments have to have a special minister, usually a priest, to confer the grace of the sacrament. But, where the sacrament of marriage is concerned, the priest is only the witness of the event. The sacrament of marriage is conferred by each of the spouses to each other. They are the ministers, conferring God's grace by themselves. 'The two become one flesh' now as part of the body of Christ, Paul's image for the Church itself, the family of God.

These reasons make the Church give every appearance of being unbending in its teaching on marriage and divorce. However, there are various reasons which may be given for the granting of nullity of marriage, in particular on grounds of defective consent. As Herbert Waddams explains: 'A declaration of nullity in regard to a marriage establishes that there has never been a true marriage, whatever may have appeared to be the case, and however long the parties may have lived together. Various reasons, such as defective consent or other impediments, may make a supposed marriage null' (J. Macquarrie and J. Childress eds, *A New Dictionary of Christian Ethics,* London, SCM Press, 1967, p. 428).

This presentation appears of necessity impersonal, and unrelated to individual marriage problems. For reasons of time, we have dealt with the teaching and not with its pastoral implementation. In practice, an enormous amount of time, skill and patience, together with great compassion, go to make up the marriage service of the Catholic Church today. Perhaps the most important aspect is the starting point, the belief of the couple in the indissolubility of marriage, and their determination to make their marriage work. But, if the marriage does run into difficulties, all kinds of help is available to see what can be done to sustain the relationship. If, on the other hand, despite all efforts, the marriage clearly cannot work, then professional advice from priests and from counsellors can help repair and lessen the damage.

The Catholic teaching also has proved itself immensely practical, even if not easy, down the centuries, and again was followed by the Church of England substantially right up to this present century. In today's society, where the institution of marriage itself is under threat, with all the consequent unhappiness, the corrosion has followed the ignoring of those words of the Lord, 'What God has joined together, let no one separate' (Mt 19:6b).

Q. But if a couple are not married in the eyes of the Church, does this not mean that they will never be able to receive Holy Communion?

A. Of course, as we have explained above, there may be the possibility of an annulment. This always should be discussed with a priest, to see if there is any way forward in that direction.

But we would have to admit that, in the present chaotic situation regarding marriage, divorce and people living together without being married, this means that there is quite a common situation developing where people will not be able to receive Holy Communion, at least for a time. Perhaps since the Second Vatican Council there has been an over-emphasis upon the act of going to Holy Communion, to counter the very strict attitudes prior to the sixties. Perhaps people in the Church need to realise that there are great spiritual benefits from participating in the liturgy *without* receiving Communion. Perhaps also the Christian community will accept more and more that there will be members in the congregation who will not be receiving Communion, for any number of reasons, and will accept that without any comment. A couple, or an individual with a marriage problem, who keep faithful to the Church's teaching will find the joy all the greater when in the course of time, and by the grace of God, they will be able to receive Our Lord in Holy Communion once again. And there is that prospect of greater joy still after death, when we truly become the body of Christ in heaven, without any further imperfection or division.

One of my greatest joys as a young priest was helping a couple solve their marriage problem. After some twenty years, a former partner had died, and now they were able to receive Holy Communion together for the first time. The years when they had not been able to receive Holy Communion had in fact brought them closer to Christ and now to each other. They had continually received what we used to call 'spiritual communion', a relationship with Christ without Communion, but genuine and fruitful. What a great joy it was when they received Communion for the first time together. They had successfully undergone their martyrdom, which was now over. Sometimes, it is a comfort to realise that nothing in this life lasts for ever, good or bad. Absence sometimes even makes the heart grow fonder, in the spiritual life as in any other aspect of life.

13

Virginity and celibacy

Q. The Catholic Church always seems to favour virginity and celibacy over the married state. Why is this so?

A. There are of course hundreds of thousands of Catholics today – priests, nuns, lay people in various communities and individually who live a life of consecrated celibacy and virginity. Incidentally, priests and nuns in particular hit the headlines when things go wrong sexually. But it is worth remembering that the vast majority are faithful to their calling, despite human weakness; and certainly the proportion of those who do not persevere in their celibate vocation is much less than the proportion of broken marriages today.

First, as we have seen, the Church teaches that the married state is not only holy, but, for two baptised persons, is elevated to being a Sacrament by Christ. The Church has canonised married people as saints, for instance St Thomas More.

The Church estimates both marriage and consecrated virginity as legitimate and good vocations, as the Catechism states:

1620 Both the Sacrament of Matrimony and virginity for the Kingdom of God come from the Lord himself.

It is he who gives them meaning and grants them the grace which is indispensable for living them out in conformity with his will. Esteem of virginity for the sake of the Kingdom and the Christian understanding of marriage are inseparable, and they reinforce each other:

> Whoever denigrates marriage also diminishes the glory of virginity. Whoever praises it makes virginity more admirable and resplendent. What appears good only in comparison with evil would not be truly good. The most excellent good is something even better than what is admitted to be good (St John Chrysostom).

So, we are not talking about one vocation being good and the other evil. The Wife of Bath tells her story in Geoffrey Chaucer's earthy *Canterbury Tales*. She defends her own frequent procreative activities, within marriage of course, insisting that St Paul only counselled virginity ('maydenhede'), and did not command it:

> For hadde God comanded maydenhede,
> Thanne hadde he dampned weddyng with the ded,
> And certes, if ther were no seed ysow,
> Virginitee, thanne whereof sholde it growe?

F.N. Robinson, ed.
The Complete Works of Geoffrey Chaucer, 2nd edition,
Oxford University Press, 1974, p. 76

Even if your Middle English is as poor as mine, you will no doubt understand what the good woman is saying. Quite simply, she says that if God had made virginity a commandment rather than a counsel, then you would have had no virgins because they would never have been born! This is a logic which could hardly be faulted.

Both marriage and virginity for the Kingdom of Heaven

are good. Rather, we are talking about two good ways of life, and the *advantage* of one over the other.

Second, the Church teaches that only those who are called to the state of celibacy or virginity should follow that way. The Church will often advise those preparing to take vows of virginity not to do so. Of course, many people will remain single, sometimes by their own decision; and lead a happy life in that state! But, for the Church to ratify a person in their calling to a state of consecrated virginity or celibacy, a period of preparation is required, often of some years, in order that the person may clearly understand what is being undertaken, and demonstrate that they have sufficient maturity to take such a vow with some chance of success.

But why take such a vow in the first place? St Paul again puts the classical position in favour of celibacy or virginity:

> I want you to be free from anxieties. The unmarried man is anxious about the affairs of the Lord, how to please the Lord; but the married man is anxious about the affairs of the world, how to please his wife, and his interests are divided. And the unmarried woman and the virgin are anxious about the affairs of the Lord, so that they may be holy in body and spirit; but the married woman is anxious about the affairs of the world, how to please her husband. I say this for your own benefit, not to put any restraint upon you, but to promote good order and unhindered devotion to the Lord.
>
> 1 Corinthians 7:32-35

Some scholars have argued, as we have seen, that Paul only counsels this way because he thinks that the end of the world is coming, so why marry? But the Church has always seen a deeper argument here: that a person who is unmarried will have fewer worldly worries, and will have more time and commitment for the Lord.

St Thomas puts the classical argument for virginity and celibacy in his *Summa Theologiae,* 2-2, q. 152, a.4. He first gives the example of Jesus and of Mary, both living a life of virginity, as an example. There he sets out the reason why in Christian tradition 'Virginity is more excellent than Matrimony':

Firstly, because a divine good is to be preferred to a human good. Secondly, because the good of the soul is to be preferred to the good of the body. And thirdly, because the good of the contemplative life is to be preferred to the good of the active life. For virginity is ordered to the good of the soul in that it is to 'think those things which are of God. But marriage is ordered to the good of the body, insofar as it is ordered to the multiplication of the human race; and it relates to the active life, in that a man and a woman who are living together as married must of necessity 'think of those things which are of the world', as the apostle says (1 Cor 7:33-4). Therefore without doubt virginity is to be preferred to a life of faithful marriage.

Aquinas is thinking as a good scholastic. If we do something, we do it for a purpose. The higher the purpose, the higher the vocation. Aquinas is saying that to go for virginity is to go Route One to God, because God is being chosen as the direct object of our desire. This links up with our very first chapter, where we spoke of the desire for God as being the ultimate aim of life, and the Commandment, to love the Lord our God with all our heart and soul as the first and greatest commandment. St Thomas is arguing that one who chooses the life of virginity is choosing God as the direct object of love, as a kind of marriage of God, even forgoing the legitimate love of marriage for this ultimate end. That is why the service of the consecration of virgins contains the symbolism of marriage, and the nun as the Bride of Christ.

Now, would he not argue that a married person who is a Christian marries for a spiritual reason, that that is best for their soul? He would not deny that. For a person who has a vocation to marry, to remain unmarried would be bad for the state of their soul. That person would lose the help marriage would give to their spiritual life, being faithful to one spouse, and growing in holiness through bringing up children. For them, marriage is preferable and more excellent than virginity.

St Thomas, then, is speaking about vocation in itself (*per se*). He is not saying that virginity is preferable for this or that person. Whatever is preferable for a given person is what helps their growth as a Christian (the technical word here is 'sanctification', that process whereby we become more like Christ). But, considered as a vocation, *per se,* the direct route to God is to be preferred to what we might call the 'worldly' or 'indirect'. Jesus said as much to Martha, as she reproved her sister Mary for contemplating at the feet of Jesus rather than helping in the kitchen:

> Now as they went on their way, Jesus entered a village; and a woman named Martha received him into her house. And she had a sister called Mary, who sat at the Lord's feet and listened to his teaching. But Martha was distracted with much serving; and she went to him and said, 'Lord, do you not care that my sister has left me to serve alone? Tell her then to help me.' But the Lord answered her, 'Martha, Martha, you are anxious and troubled about many things; one thing is needful. Mary has chosen the good portion, which shall not be taken away from her.'
>
> Luke 10:38-42

Q. But if we all followed this way, surely there would be no children born into the world?

A. This is the Wife of Bath's argument again. That would

be so if everyone chose a life of virginity. But you do not think that will ever happen, do you? The majority of people will choose to serve God in their neighbour, through the institution of marriage. People who are guided by God in their lives will usually choose that vocation anyway. God will take care of the population of the human race! Also, as we said earlier, the institution of marriage is strengthened by people who are consecrated to a life of virginity, by their example and by their help. Think of the thousands of people helped by those consecrated to God in religious orders dedicated to nursing and to education; and of course those helped by celibate priests.

The Church has always linked virginity with the other two 'Evangelical (i.e. Gospel) counsels' (not commandments, you will note), poverty and obedience:

> *Poverty* is the Evangelical counsel which leads a person to give up even legitimate ownership of property to become rich in the Kingdom of Heaven.

> *Virginity* (usually called *chastity*; but, as we have seen, a person can be truly chaste within marriage) is the Evangelical counsel which leads a person to give up even legitimate commitment to another person in marriage to be freer to love God as the direct object of desire.

> *Obedience* is the Evangelical counsel which leads a person to give up the freedom of their own decision to follow whatever is decided by their own religious community.

Of the three counsels, the most difficult often is the third, obedience! In the popular film, *The Nun's Story,* the heroine decides to join a religious order which runs medical services on the missions. Her father tries to dissuade her. 'My dear', he says, 'I can see you able to take the vow of poverty, even of chastity; but I cannot see you able to follow obedience.' As the story turns out, her father was right. After becoming a nun, she went out to the missions, and resisted the temptation offered by a handsome agnostic surgeon. But eventually she found irreconcilable conflict between her professional life as a nurse and the requirements of her order to keep the discipline of community and prayer life.

It cannot be repeated too often that poverty, chastity and obedience are vows only for those called to that way of life; as Jesus said himself regarding eunuchs 'for the Kingdom of Heaven's sake', 'Let anyone accept this who can' (Mt 19:10-12).

Nor should we be bothered as Christians to rate someone else as leading a higher vocation than ourselves. As Paul says, we are all members of the same body. We do not have all the same function. Mother Teresa, the twentieth-century saint who nursed the poor and dying in India, founding a famous worldwide Order and becoming friend to popes and national leaders such as Princess Diana, died leaving a bucket as her only possession, for her clothes to be washed in. In following that life of poverty, she was closer to Christ than the rest of us with our mortgages and credit cards. Why should we bother if the Church rates her vocation of poverty as in itself higher than those who live in the world and possess the world's goods, if she has given up all personal wealth for Christ? What is wrong with reckoning someone else as better than ourselves?

Q. I thought that you have said that the vow of virginity or celibacy is voluntary. Why then does the Church insist upon celibacy for the priest?

A. Regarding Catholic priests being celibate, it should be clear to everyone that this is only a disciplinary law, not a question of doctrine. In fact, there always have been married priests in the Catholic Church, in particular in those parts of the Catholic Church which do not follow the Western discipline, but are for example, Russian, Greek or Syriac in their discipline (called 'Uniate', i.e. united with Rome, in distinction with the 'Eastern Orthodox' separate from Rome). In those communities, the same rule applies as in the Orthodox churches, namely that a married man can become a priest, although a priest cannot marry after ordination.

Furthermore, in England and in the USA recently there have been a number of married men, ex-Anglican ordained presbyters, who have been ordained as Roman Catholic priests. Nothing in theory would prevent such a practice spreading wider. The Church acknowledges that many married priests act faithfully and well in their priestly ministry. Those of us who live in countries where the churches of the Reformation tradition are strong will testify to excellent ministers of the Gospel whose wives and families share with them in their pastoral ministry.

However, when the question of changing the law of priestly celibacy was raised at the Second Vatican Council, the bishops strongly agreed to retain the present discipline that the Western Church would continue only to ordain those as priest who were prepared to make a promise of perpetual celibacy. It is at least worth looking at one paragraph of the *Decree on the Ministry and Life of Priests* to note the reasons why the bishops were so firm in their conclusion to retain priestly celibacy:

Celibacy is in very many ways appropriate to the priesthood. For the whole mission of a priest is a dedication to the service of the new humanity, which Christ who triumphed over death brings into being in the world by his Spirit, and which draws its origin 'not of blood nor of the will of the flesh nor of the will of man, but of God' (Jn 1:13). Through virginity or celibacy preserved for the sake of the Kingdom of Heaven, priests are consecrated to Christ in a new and exalted manner, and more easily cleave to him with singleness

133

of heart; in him and through him they devote themselves with greater freedom to the service of God and people; they are more untrammelled in serving his Kingdom and his work of heavenly regeneration; and thus they are more equipped to accept a wider fatherhood in Christ. By this state they make an open profession to people that they desire to devote themselves with undivided loyalty to the task entrusted to them, namely to betroth the faithful to one husband and present them as a pure bride to Christ, and so they appeal to that mysterious marriage, brought into being by God and to be openly revealed in time to come, in which the church has Christ as her only husband. They become, indeed, a living sign that the world to come, in which the children of the resurrection will neither marry nor be given in marriage, is already present among us through faith and love.

Vatican II, Decree on the Ministry and Life of Priests, *Presbyterorum Ordinis,* No. 160. Tanner, II, *PO,* p. 1062, lines 28 to 1063, line 5.

For many of us priests, while the above words from the Decree sometimes look impossibly idealistic, they do represent a pastoral vision which is inspiring and has encouraged us throughout our priestly lives. In sum, therefore, the Council argues that, while celibacy is not of the essence of the priesthood (its *esse),* nevertheless it is of its well-being (its *bene esse*).

There is happiness too in the kind of commitment which the celibacy of the priest required, a commitment to Christ and to his Church. To attain mastery of oneself, body and soul is a lifetime process. But at least I can say again, with thousands of other priests, that I am not only by the grace of God a celibate priest; I am also a happy one. The journey, the hard work, is worth it. Married couples who have remained faithful to their calling will say the same. This is not a denial of our freedom to be required to take the vow of celibacy. No one has the right to ordination. The Church requires this sacrifice as a qualification for our ordination.

Q. But I still cannot understand why you have to insist upon the Church's teaching that virginity or celibacy is preferable to marriage. Are not we all equal in God's sight, whatever our vocation?

A. Yes, of course we are. And, as I said, for some people it would be quite wrong not to marry, because that is their vocation. But we do need to insist upon the Church's teaching at this point, that virginity is a higher vocation than marriage, just as that poverty is a higher vocation than accepting a life of ownership, and that obedience is a higher way of life than choosing what we do as individuals.

This is because poverty, virginity and obedience look forward to the life we shall lead after death. When we die, we shall take nothing with us; we shall be completely poor, as naked as the day we were born. We will leave our husbands and wives behind. We will not be able to decide to do anything, we will be completely unable to act at all, as a corpse. We will truly have poverty, virginity and obedience.

But the Church teaches that that is the beginning of real life, not its end. That is when we shall see God, by his grace and our co-operation throughout this life. That happiness in God will burn away every other desire, or rather take up every desire into that divine vision. We will need neither property nor spouse, nor will there be conflicts as to what to do. As Jesus said, 'The sons of this age marry and are given in marriage; but those who are accounted worthy to attain to that age and to the resurrection from the dead neither marry nor are given in marriage, for they cannot die any more, because they are equal to angels and are sons of God, being sons of the resurrection' (Lk 20:34-6 RSV).

This life is a preparation for that life to come. Married couples say that, even if they are close to each other in a happy union, each one needs 'space'. They help each other yet need to be alone also. There is something of the monk in all of us. The word 'monk' means one who is alone with God *(monachos)*. Marriage is a happy life, but a poor idol. Perhaps one problem in the modern world is that marriage is seen as Eldorado, happy ever after, a Hollywood dream world.

The modern world has spawned the horrific tales of Don Juan and Casanova, completely promiscuous men in league with the devil. Marriage can bring happiness, if the couple and the children work at it. But it cannot bring paradise. Don Juan, (or Don Giovanni in Mozart's opera) can never find ultimate happiness in one woman, therefore he must search for another, and another, and another. Is that also the horror of the legend of Bluebeard, the man who lures women to his castle only to put them to death and adore them as statues? Christian revelation tells Casanova, Don Juan and Bluebeard that only God can satisfy their craving for ultimate happiness, for the infinite. The Christian faith sees marriage as the way ordained by God, but only for this life. In heaven, our union with God, and with each other as human beings, will be greater even than sexual union between a happy couple. That sexual union on earth is a sign of that future ecstasy which we all hope and pray for. Some humans have the vocation to enjoy the sign in order together by God's grace to attain the reality. Others are called to ignore the sign and go for the reality while on earth, using the helps God gives.

14

Falling in love is wonderful

They say that falling in love is wonderful,
is marvellous.
That's what they say.

So proclaimed the old hit song: and who could possibly disagree ? Of all the experiences of life, falling in love is perhaps the most beautiful. The person in love feels that after all this life is worth while. Everything that happened before, life before love, was purely mundane, boring. Now everything falls into place. This life means the other person.

The Church teaches that falling in love is a great gift of God. God wants us to be happy in this life as well as in the next. And God wants that happiness to be in our relationships with other human beings. One of the most important relationships is the union between a man and woman in marriage. Falling in love is the usual way in which a couple bond with each other emotionally, in a time of courtship, in order to prepare themselves for life together, with all its ups and downs, hopefully fruitful in bringing into this world new human beings in that same love.

In the first chapter of this book, we quoted the Song of Solomon, one of the most beautiful erotic poems in literary history; and it is in the Bible! It is important to repeat that the Church believes that the Bible is the Word of God, God's written message for us humans.

In the Church's teaching, God is the true author of the Bible; but God did not dispense with the human writers, using them as mere machines. Rather, as the Second Vatican Council stated in 1965: 'To compose the sacred books, God chose certain people who, all the while he employed them in this task, made full use of their powers and faculties so that, though he acted in them and by them, it was as true authors that they consigned to writing whatever he wanted written, and no more' (Dogmatic Constitution on Divine Revelation, *Dei Verbum,* No. 11).

That means, does it not, that God used *the feelings* of those writers. Clearly, the writer of the Song of Solomon knows what it is to be in love, or has an extraordinary ability to enter into human emotions. The writer of the Song of Solomon expresses the beautiful call of the young lover to his beloved to go away with him to make love:

> My beloved speaks and says to me: 'Arise, my love, my fair one, and come away; for now the winter is past, the rain is over and gone.
> The flowers appear on the earth; the time of singing has come, and the voice of
> the turtledove is heard in our land.
> The fig tree puts forth its figs, and the vines are in blossom; they give forth fragrance. Arise, my love, my fair one, and come away.
> O my dove, in the clefts of the rock, in the covert of the cliff, let me see your face, let me hear your voice; for your voice is sweet, and your face is lovely.'
>
> Song of Solomon 2:10-14

The author is celebrating here the falling in love of a man and a woman. Even more, as again we have seen in the first chapter of this book, the sexual attraction between them is an essential part of that falling in love. The man desires to kiss the woman's lips, to press her breasts. The woman adores her man's strong body, seeing his testicles like jewels set in his navel. All this the author of this ancient biblical poem not only records, but celebrates, sharing the feelings of those young lovers. Some scholars even think that the poems might have been written by the lovers themselves! That is not impossible, although it is impossible to prove.

Finally, the Song of Solomon goes the whole way. It does not even stop at celebrating falling in love. It actually describes the desire for the sexual act itself, using only thinly veiled language:

> I am my beloved's, and his desire is for me.
> Come, my beloved, let us go forth into the fields, and lodge in the villages; let us go out early to the vineyards, and see whether the vines have budded, whether the grape blossoms have opened and the pomegranates are in bloom.
> There I will give you my love.
> The mandrakes give forth fragrance, and over our doors are all choice fruits, new as well as old, which I have laid up for you, O my beloved.
>
> Song of Solomon 7:10-13

The old Catholic Douay version of the Bible is even bolder. It says there I will give thee my breasts' rather than 'There I will give you my love'. The parts of the body have already been described in the poem as fruits, the woman's breasts as clusters of grapes (7:8). Thus the woman invites her man to share in those fruits in an act of sexual love. Mandrakes, as we all know, are primitive aphrodisiacs. It seems that when the poem speaks of 'gates' or 'doors', the author intends to refer to the sexual organs themselves. It is difficult to see another meaning for the following verses:

I slept, but my heart was awake. Listen! my beloved is knocking. 'Open to me, my sister, my love, my dove, my perfect one; for my head is wet with dew, my locks with the drops of the night.'

I had put off my garment; how could I put it on again? I had bathed my feet; how could I soil them?

My beloved thrust his hand into the opening, and my inmost being yearned for him.

I arose to open to my beloved, and my hands dripped with myrrh, my fingers with liquid myrrh, upon the handles of the bolt.

I opened to my beloved, but my beloved had turned and was gone. My soul failed me when he spoke. I sought him, but did not find him; I called him, but he gave no answer.

Song of Solomon 5:2-6

The meaning of the text here, it seems clear to some scholars, is that the author is describing the sexual act itself in symbolic language. The woman has undressed for her beloved; she has washed her feet (a Hebrew euphemism for the sexual organs); she opens for her lover to thrust into her vagina, her 'door'. She is 'wet' for him. Unfortunately, he does not complete the act, but goes away. She yearns for the fullness of that love, of that sexual act, and is desperate to find him again.

It is right for us to spend some time on this poem, because it is necessary to emphasise that the Church itself, in proclaiming that this poem is part of the Bible, 'canonises' falling in love, and indeed its fullness of expression in the act of sexual intercourse. As we saw above, in the chapter on the sexual organs, God has made us sexual beings, in order to provide the physical dynamism for the union between man and woman, which itself has the purpose of providing the growth of the human race in love. We must quote Genesis again. God, in the primitive story, is looking for a companion for the man he has just created.

The animals just are not good enough:

> So the LORD God caused a deep sleep to fall upon the man, and he slept; then he took one of his ribs and closed up its place with flesh. And the rib that the LORD God had taken from the man he made into a woman and brought her to the man. Then the man said, 'This at last is bone of my bones and flesh of my flesh; this one shall be called Woman, for out of Man this one was taken.'
>
> Therefore a man leaves his father and his mother and clings to his wife, and they become one flesh. And the man and his wife were both naked, and were not ashamed.
>
> Genesis 2:21-25

Thus falling in love between a man and a woman, when seen in its proper light, is part of God's plan of love for the human race. This is not only to propagate the human race. It is much more to fill it with true human and divine love. It is the divine dynamism which exists in the human being to attract one man to one woman through the powerful passions which are both spiritual and physical.

How beautiful it is to see a young couple, head over heels in love with each other, giving themselves to each other for life. Even more beautiful it is when you see that couple fifty years later, at their golden wedding anniversary, still very much in love. Falling in love when they first met was the flame which lit their love for each other, which flame did not burn out, but became a steady glow to warm not only themselves but their children and their grandchildren and their friends. As the Pope said recently, they have ignited a mini-church, a family, founded on God's love, their love for each other, and Christ's love for them and their love for him.

Q. Then what is the problem? The Bible likes people to fall in love. Why not just let them get on with it?

A. We all know that it is not as easy as that. In the first chapter of this book, we referred to the awful story of the rape of Dinah (Gen 34:34-41). Her brothers took terrible vengeance by killing men, women and children of her tribe. The man who raped her had nevertheless fallen in love with her, and wanted her for his wife. But the fact that he had originally raped her called forth that horrific retribution.

Remember also that we quoted from the same Song of Solomon which had just praised the falling in love of a young man and woman:

> 'Love is as strong as death,
> passion cruel as the grave;
> it blazes up like blazing fire,
> fiercer than any flame.
> Many waters cannot quench love,
> no flood can sweep it away.

Song of Solomon 8:6b-7

The problem is that we have a disordered nature as the result of Original Sin, the fault of our first parents. We cannot go fully into this doctrine here and now. The reader is referred for a fuller yet a very basic treatment in the *Catechism of the Catholic Church,* or to my own publications *Faith Alive* (with Rowanne Pasco, Hodder and Stoughton 1994) or more recently *Catholic Basics* (Universe Publications 1999).

The doctrine of the Church is that, as the result of the sin of our first parents, we have a nature which has been wounded. We have lost the right relationship with God with which we were created; and, as a result, our passions are difficult to control. As Paul himself said, after many years of faithful Christian service, he still had a problem:

> So I find it to be a law that when I want to do what is good, evil lies close at hand... but I see in my members

142

another law at war with the law of my mind and making me captive to the law of sin that dwells in my members. Wretched man that I am! Who will deliver me from this body of death?

Romans 7:21-24

The Christian doctrine is that, Christ, by his life, death and resurrection, has destroyed the power of evil in us. By baptism, Christians are given the life of God and the gift of the Holy Spirit to restore that relationship with God lost at the Fall. But the effects of Original Sin in our wounded nature still remain. It is as if a patient has been cured of a deadly illness by an extensive operation; but that patient is left weak and vulnerable, and will have some time of convalescence. The weakness which still remains is called by the Church 'concupiscence', that disordered nature which is the result of Original Sin, and which remains even after baptism, as Paul himself says above. Our life remains therefore a daily contest with our disordered nature, to become what we are, truly like Christ through the working of the Holy Spirit. Again, Paul puts it perfectly:

But if we have died with Christ, we believe that we will also live with him. We know that Christ, being raised from the dead will never die again; death no longer has dominion over him. The death he died he died to sin, once for all; but the life he lives, he lives to God. So you also must consider yourselves dead to sin and alive to God in Christ Jesus. Therefore do not let sin exercise dominion in your mortal bodies, to make you obey their passions (*epithumia*). No longer present your members to sin as instruments of wickedness, but present yourselves to God as those who have been brought from death to life, and present your members to God as instruments of righteousness.

Romans 6:8-13

143

The Greek word *epithumia* (all the New Testament was written in Greek) means 'disordered passions'. Paul says that we cannot just obey our passions. That does not mean, of course, that we never have to follow our feelings. The young couple who fall madly in love may follow their passions without any guilt, if they are free to marry. They are free not only to follow their passions, but even to further stimulate them on their wedding night. But the man who falls madly in love with his new shapely secretary cannot follow his passions if he has a wife and three children at home, to break his solemn vows to his wife and to disrupt the lives of his children. 'Falling in love' can never be a justification to do what is wrong, to break God's commandments. That is what Paul means above.

The difficulty today is that, in our contemporary culture, feelings have themselves become a justification for action, without any concern for what is morally right and wrong independently of those feelings. If I feel it, I can do it. Throughout the history of the world, throughout the two thousand years of Christianity, people have done what is wrong, done what is wrong sexually. They have committed fornication, adultery, homosexual acts, even bestiality. What is different today is that many people do not consider that such acts are wrong. If they have 'fallen in love', that is justification for the act, without any further moral criteria whereby that act must be judged.

We have already seen that, in a contraceptive society such as ours, the link between sex and procreation has been broken, with subsequent sexual anarchy. There is a further factor which we have yet to explain. That is what we might call the 'romantic' factor, which influences our thinking at all levels and in every aspect of our lives.

We are all heirs of the Enlightenment, that philosophical movement of the eighteenth century which enthroned reason as the ultimate human value. The Western world had already by that time made huge advances in science, using Newtonian physics. It was felt that this natural science would in the end explain everything. Religion would be *passé,* a relic of the superstitious past, unless that religion could justify itself at the bar of reason, i.e. in terms of the new science. The idea of some truth being beyond the scope of natural science, 'metaphysics' as it was traditionally called, 'beyond physics', was entirely unacceptable to the Enlightenment world-view. Thus the idea of Christian revelation, of truth communicated directly by God, especially the idea of miracles and the incarnation, God becoming Man in Jesus, such an idea was a prime example of such *a passé* concept past its sell-by date.

But paradoxically, as so often happens in history where the unexpected tends to occur, in attempting to enthrone reason, the philosophy of the Enlightenment simply succeeded in dethroning it. Perhaps the most influential philosopher of the Enlightenment, and indeed perhaps the most influential philosopher of the modern world, was Immanuel Kant, a German Pietist. Pietism was a radical form of Protestantism, which emphasised the spirit in the individual (Pietism is approximately represented in its Anglo-Saxon form as Quakerism). Dogmas of faith were considered by Pietism to be unnecessary. What mattered was the Spirit of God working in the interior life of the individual. Pietism was therefore an ideal religion for the Enlightenment, dispensing with the necessity of the old 'supernatural truths' such as expressed in the Christian Creed.

Kant's most famous work was *A Critique of Pure Reason.* Kant's purpose was to prove that human reason is too subjective to be able to know objective truth. It cannot discover metaphysical truths such as proving that God exists by the old arguments of cause and effect, or even proving that a world exists external to ourselves. Kant, following the extreme empiricism of the Scottish philosopher David Hume, held that we do not know objective reality through our senses. All we have is a series of sensations, one following the other with great rapidity and variety. In saying 'this is a world', 'this is a cat', 'this is a football match', 'I have a pain in my stomach', we are taking sensations and giving them 'categories' such as time, space, extension, shape. We do not know what is in reality (what Kant called the *noumena),* we only know the appearances, reality as it appears to us (what he called *the phenomena).* Kant has thereby almost reduced the world to what the computer industry would call today 'virtual reality'!

For Kant, we only know that God exists through the moral sense of obligation (the 'ought' as he called it).But this sense of 'ought' would seem to have no objective referent, only our own subjective sense of it. Kant attempted to prove that this sense of obligation must exist, because it could not just come from ourselves. But his 'moral argument for the existence of God', not surprisingly, suffered the same fate within the philosophical world following Kant as the arguments for God's existence from cause and effect did in his own system! How can we know the objective truth of our moral sense if we cannot know even the objective truth of the physical world about us – trees, fields, houses, philosophers giving lectures?

Kant, as I have said, was enormously influential in the modern world. He could even be called *the* philosopher of the modern age. It is not surprising, therefore, that, as night follows day and the nineteenth century followed the eighteenth, reason gave way to feeling as the ultimate human value in philosophy. Indeed, not only in philosophy, but in every area of European culture, particularly in art, music, and literature, to feel something was the ultimate criterion of morality. Since reason had been critiqued by the philosophical guru of the modern world, Immanuel Kant, what further check could there be on the onward march of feeling?

Of course, those who promoted Romanticism in the nineteenth century (because that was what this new movement was called, from the word *roman,* novel) would strenuously argue that not just any feeling would do to be self-justifying. The German philosophers and *literati* used the word *Gefühle,* which means very much more than 'feeling'. Perhaps 'experience' would be a better rendering of *Gefühle*. But the subsequent problem is not far to fathom. If reason can no longer be used as a criterion for discovering what is objectively true, how are we to discern one feeling from another; a 'good feeling' from a 'bad feeling', a 'profound feeling' from a 'superficial feeling', a 'right feeling' from a 'wrong feeling'?

The Romantic philosophy has had a huge impact on our contemporary world. Nineteenth-century Romanticism influenced in particular the great German music of that century, particularly perhaps the most influential musician in the history of the world, Richard Wagner. Wagner's musical revolution, the change from the more formal harmonies of Bach, Mozart, and even of Beethoven, to a much more emotionally free and structurally flexible harmonic system based on chromatic progressions, has revolutionised the music of this century, not only classical music, but pop music as well. The mega music industry of today is the offspring of Wagner, whether it likes it or not.

The myths in the story-lines of Wagner's operas (or, as he would prefer to call them, his 'music dramas' are likewise heavily influenced by Romanticism. Wagner rewrote all the legends he used as the basis of his music dramas. The famous cycle of four operas *Das Ring der Nibelungen* (The Nibelungs Ring) is loosely based on the German legend of the hero Siegfried. But Wagner creates his own legend through his own story-line.

At the opening scene of *Die Walküre,* Sieglinde the wife of Hunding is surprised by the entry of a fugitive Siegmund. She falls in love with this stranger, who is the Wagnerian hero of *Die Walküre.* The opera obviously encourages us to think that there is nothing wrong with her adulterous relationship with Siegmund, nor with the fact that Siegmund is Sieglinde's own brother, their relationship thus being also incestuous! On the contrary, Siegmund sings his rapturous love-song to Sieglinde, 'Oh wondrous vision! Rapturous woman!'

Clearly, the feelings are self-justifying. Wagner encourages us to think that Hunding is a cad anyway, and has no right to Sieglinde's love, even though they are married.

The music dramas of Wagner incorporate all that is best and all that is worst in the Romantic movement. A very destructive philosophy of life is presented in what some consider to be the most superb orchestral and vocal music ever written, and certainly the most seductive. Magnificent music, but terrible philosophy.

The Romantic movement has become a billion-dollar industry in the twentieth century, based at Hollywood, California, USA. Wagner's operas continue to draw a fanatical following, from those who can afford the tickets at Bayreuth, Covent Garden or the Metropolitan Opera House, New York. But where Wagner continues to play to his thousands, Hollywood spreads Romanticism to millions, indeed to billions, of people through cinemas, televisions and video hire shops throughout the world.

Hollywood's great heresy is the self-justification of falling in love. (I speak as one who loves the cinema, incidentally, and has had great entertainment from many good films throughout my life.) When a couple fall in love in a film drama, that is in itself right, whatever the consequences, proclaims the dogmatic creed of Hollywood. Take for example *Falling in Love,* starring Meryl Streep and Robert de Niro. These top film actors play two middleclass commuters travelling on the train to work each day. Both he and she are happily married with good jobs and children. But the inevitable happens: they fall in love.

The film narrates how they meet for meals, then begin to delay home-coming in the evening with their liaisons, and finally how they fall into bed together in a local motel. Eventually, both have to spill the beans to their spouses. The consequences are naturally disastrous: the destruction of their family life, all vividly presented in well-played scenes.

But Hollywood can only have one ending to *Falling in*

Love. He (Robert de Niro) makes a resolution to return to his wife and family. That is his responsibility, he says. Yet, in terms of Hollywood philosophy, such resolutions are vain in the light of the demands of passion. The final scene is once more on the daily commuter train. Their eyes meet, and they know that, despite all the rules, they must pursue their love. The film ends with their embrace. Falling in love has won again.

For me, however, and perhaps for others in that cinema, *Falling in Love* must be said to have a disappointing ending. Who are we to think of most? Is it the two lovers, obeying their passion? Or are we allowed to spare a thought for their spouses and children, their lives now broken and their love for their father or mother betrayed?

Clearly, Romanticism makes good film footage. Robert de Niro going back to his wife would not make commercial cinema. The powerful images of the motion picture are particularly well suited to the love-is-all philosophy. But, for those of us who have to live our lives in the real world and not on the cinema screen, how are we to make sense of falling in love, and make the right decisions, sometimes with, and sometimes against, our feelings?

15

Falling in love: what is love?

Q. How are we to make sense of falling in love and make the right decisions, sometimes with, and sometimes against, our feelings? What is love?

A. To answer the question as to how to make the right decision regarding falling in love, we must first ask what it is to love. In classical Catholic theology, love is a passion. This is from the Latin word *pati*, to suffer. The Latin, word for 'suffer' does not necessarily mean to suffer pain, but to suffer anything, good or evil. *A passion is something which happens to us*. Furthermore, it happens in our 'sensitive appetite' as the scholastics called it. It happens in our senses, in our physical feelings:

> 1763 The term 'passions' belongs to the Christian patrimony. Feelings or passions are emotions or movements of the sensitive appetite that incline us to act or not to act in regard to something felt or imagined to be good or evil.

> 1764 The passions are natural components of the human psyche; they form the passageway and ensure the connection between the life of the senses and the life of the mind. Our Lord called man's heart the source from which the passions spring.

That is why we call it *falling* in love, like tripping over a stone. We did not mean it to happen!

So far, all would no doubt agree. Falling in love is something which happens to human beings. Love is a passion; so are anger, fear and pride. Like these other passions, the classical or scholastic theology states that passions are our feelings. We can in that sense do nothing about them. They are not in themselves right or wrong; they just happen.

But passions can nevertheless be judged morally, considered in the light of our reason, which can choose to encourage or not to encourage them. As St Thomas Aquinas says in his *Summa Theologica*, 1-2 q.24, a.1, 'If we consider passions in relation to the fact that they are subject to the command of our reason and our will, so we can say that those passions are either good or evil.'

In this sense, the lust for another man's wife is an evil passion. So is wilful hatred for another person. It is one of those passions (*epithumia*) which, as St Peter says, 'war against the soul'; even if it is 'natural' in the sense that it happened to the man involved. Nevertheless, says Aquinas, if it is inclining him to do something which is in itself morally wrong, then that passion can itself be adjudged to be evil. Thus Sieglinde's incestuous passion for Siegmund, and his for her, would be in this Thomistic sense be adjudged to be an evil passion. As such, the person to whom that passion is happening must control it, and not give in to the demands of that passion.

Therefore, as the Catechism says:

1767 In themselves passions are neither good nor evil. They are morally qualified only to the extent that they effectively engage reason and will. Passions are said to be voluntary, 'either because they are commanded by the will or because the will does not place obstacles in their way'. It belongs to the perfection of the moral or human good that the passions be governed by reason.

'Of course, sometimes for St Thomas reason dictates that passions are for an entirely good purpose and should be stimulated. Such would be the passion of a married couple for each other. At the right time, when they make love, they should really enjoy it. Thomas even argues that it is better morally for a person to act both with feeling and with reason, than to act without feeling. Thomas argues this against the Greek Stoic philosophers, who thought that any passion diminished moral goodness, which should be governed by reason alone without any feeling. On the contrary, says Aquinas:

> It is better that a person should not only want the good, but also to do it by external action. Therefore it follows that it is better for human perfection that a person should be motivated towards the good not only with the will, but also with the sensitive appetite; as it is said in Psalm 83:3: *My heart and my flesh rejoice in the living God.* By *heart* we understand the intellectual appetite, by flesh we understand the sensitive appetite (1-2 q.24 a.3).

Therefore, says Thomas, if we moderate passion by reason, then our passions can increase the goodness of our moral actions. The flesh is by no means evil, unless acting contrary to reason.

Q. But what has love to do with reason? Surely, as the Beatles said, 'all you need is love'. There is nothing here about reason!

A. There is a sense in which the Beatles, the Liverpudlian pop group who took the sixties by storm, are right here. 'All you need is love.' This slogan is not too different from what the fourth-century Christian saint and theologian Augustine of Hippo said, 'Love God and do what you like.' If we love rightly, then that is all we need. But how do we love rightly? Did the stars in the film *Falling in Love* love rightly, when their love destroyed the love which each had committed to another spouse and to the children of that original love?

What, then, is true love? The Catechism gives the definition of Christian tradition:

> 1766 'To love is to will the good of another.' All other affections have their source in this first movement of the human heart toward the good. Only the good can be loved. Passions 'are evil if love is evil and good if it is good'.

We have seen that all passion is rooted in the 'sensitive appetite'. We are beings with a physical body, and that body has feelings. But human passion is also based upon the 'intellective appetite'. That is to say, as created with an immortal soul by God, we desire the good which is apprehended by our mind. We freely then choose that good. We are not simply driven by instinct, as the animals. That element of the choice of the good, as opposed to being the slave of our instincts, is precisely what sets us off as different from the animals.

That good which we choose regarding persons is truly to love them, that is, to want their good. Aquinas divides love into two: love of desire, and love of friendship.

> So therefore the movement of love drives in two directions; first of all, towards the good which one wishes for something, or for oneself, or for others; and secondly, towards the actual person for which one wishes good. The drive towards the good which one wishes for something else, is called the love of desire; the drive towards the actual person for whom one wishes good is called the love of friendship (1-2 q.26 a.4).

A straightforward reflection upon our own experience will

tell us how perceptive is this analysis by Aquinas. Human friendship begins with love of desire. This desire (Latin *concupiscentia*) is not necessarily for sex, but for something pleasurable which a relationship gives. People realise that they like the same things. They enjoy going to the same films, eating at the same restaurant, they like their company. They 'like' each other.

But initially, they like each other only for the things which mutually cause them enjoyment. At this early stage of a friendship, it is a pleasure to be together; but, for Aquinas, this is not yet true friendship. If one person has some benefit to give the other, it may only be a question of what we call 'cupboard love'. The relationship is only founded on what either can get from the other, upon self-interest, not upon a genuine love for each other.

True friendship begins when both begin to want the best for each other, as person. It is only the second, for Aquinas, the love of friendship, which is, simply speaking, love. One person is in trouble, and discusses it at a meal with the friend. It is clear that the other person is worried, shares that trouble. They wish each other's good, and fear when the other person is suffering some kind of evil. 'Greater love has no one than this,' said Jesus, 'than when someone lays down their life for a friend' (Jn 15:13). That is truly the love of friendship. For a true friend, that desire for the good of the other person is so great that someone would die rather than see evil come upon that friend. Thus a headmaster of a school in London, when going out of his school gates, intervened to prevent one of his pupils being attacked, and was himself stabbed to death. That is the ultimate love of friendship. It was also a free choice of that headmaster, the good of the other person, not just a feeling that enjoyment was caused by doing the same things together, 'You scratch my back, I scratch yours.'

The greatest example of friendship is, of course, Jesus our Lord himself. He said to his disciples, on the evening before his arrest and crucifixion:

154

'This is my commandment, that you love one another as I have loved you. No one has greater love than this, to lay down one's life for one's friends. You are my friends if you do what I command you. I do not call you servants any longer, because the servant does not know what the master is doing; but I have called you friends, because I have made known to you everything that I have heard from my Father.

John 15:12-15

The best marriages are where the couple become the very best of friends. Marriage is the most intimate form of friendship which exists here on earth. There is that revelation of one to the other which Jesus promised his friends, his disciples. Such a couple would happily die for each other. They wish each other good; and the same deep friendship extends to their children, the fruit of their love. It is a wonderful sight, to see an old married couple entirely one with each, other, accepting each other as they are, a lifetime of togetherness.

Sex is a vital part of this relationship. Their physical union has bonded them to each other and to their children. The pleasure which they have had in sex has given them delight in each other in the most intimate way. But their relationship has developed over the years. From being a delight in the *pleasure* each has in the other, the love of desire, that marriage has become more and more a delight in each other *for* the other, the love of friendship. That is a God-designed progression of their love.

But we know that it does not always work out like this. It is relatively easy for a couple to find delight in the *pleasure* which they have for each other, particularly where they like having sex together. It is more difficult to move towards a delight in each other *for* the other, that love of friendship which in the end is the only secure foundation of a good marriage.

That is also why Christian tradition has always

155

counselled moderation in love, because love must be a commitment of the will as well as of the emotions. Shakespeare's *Romeo and Juliet* has recently, been made into a blockbuster film putting the characters in modern dress. The Franciscan Friar Laurence, in his psychedelic shirt, tries to calm Romeo and Juliet, who come to him crazy with passionate love. The good Friar warns them to cool it:

> These violent delights have violent ends,
> And in their triumph die, like fire and powder,
> Which as they kiss consume...
> Therefore love moderately; long love doth so,
> Too swift arrives as tardy as to slow.
>
> (Act 2, Scene 6)

More commendable is the moderation of Tobias, in the Old Testament, quoted in the Catechism, who is fearful of a demon destroying him and his newly wed Sarah. As we saw in Chapter 9, instead of immediately making love to his bride:

> 2361 Tobias got out of bed and said to Sarah, 'Sister, get up, and let us pray and implore our Lord that he grant us mercy and safety.' So she got up, and they began to pray and implore that they might be kept safe. Tobias began by saying, 'Blessed are you, O God of our fathers... You made Adam, and for him you made his wife Eve as a helper and support. From the two of them the race of mankind has sprung. You said, "It is not good that the man should be alone; let us make a helper for him like himself." I now am taking this kinswoman of mine, not because of lust, but with sincerity. Grant that she and I may find mercy and that we may grow old together.' And they both said, 'Amen, Amen.' Then they went to sleep for the night.
>
> Tobit 8:4-9

Tobias and Sarah were practising married chastity. Their making love at the right time, later, would be all the more pleasurable to them, because they had put God first before their passion for each other. They would be rewarded by true love, both of body and of spirit.

That is also why marriage groups such as Marriage Encounter, where married couples meet to grow together in their married relationship, are so helpful. Such groups enable couples to reflect on their relationship, perhaps after a good number of years together, to grow towards that willing for each other's good which is the only foundation for a happy marriage.

But can any human relationship develop from love of sexual desire to love of friendship? Can a homosexual relationship develop in this way? Can a relationship between a married person and an unmarried be anything else than adulterous? Can a celibate stay with a person as a friend when passion is powerful? Now we arrive at perhaps the most thorny of questions!

16

Falling in love: sex and friendship,
to stay or to run?

Q. The modern world envisages many kinds of permanent relationship as valid, with a sexual element. Cannot any of these relationships lead to genuine friendship?

A. This is again a question of how we look at what genuine love is, and genuine friendship. If love is to will someone else good, the love of friendship as we saw in the previous chapter, then we can only be true friends if we want for them something which is genuinely good. That may not necessarily be something which they themselves, see as good. It must be something which is really good for them.

You may have a friend who is an alcoholic. That friend has been off drink, 'dry', for two years. He goes to a stag party. His pals there challenge him to be really macho, and have a drink like the rest of the boys, just this once, at the party. He is sorely tempted. He desperately *wants* a drink. But you know that this will set him off down the path to ruin once more. You edge him out of the party, and get him away in your car. He agrees. That is being a real friend to him.

You see the point. A true friend will want what is genuinely good for a friend, not even what that friend

158

might think he or she wants at a particular time. Of course, this can be taken too far. Being a friend also means understanding the eccentricities of the other person. A true friend will even stay around when that friend has done something which he or she knows is not good for them. That friend will stay around when there is a minor difference of opinion over food or clothes or entertainment. But a friend will want the true good for the other person, not the counterfeit.

Now, what is truly good? We saw earlier that the human mind, the human heart, longs for what is truly good. Ultimately, that good is the Infinite Good, God himself. 'Love God and love your neighbour as yourself.' That is the twofold command. That good is also the creatures God has made for us and for God's glory. We repeat the Catechism definition we quoted earlier:

> 1766 'To love is to will the good of another.' All other affections have their source in this first movement of the human heart toward the good. Only the good can be loved. Passions 'are evil if love is evil and good if it is good'.

That means that we cannot truly love a person if we co-operate with them in what is intrinsically evil. We mentioned in an earlier chapter that, according to Catholic morality, there are some moral acts which are of themselves evil, and can never be under any circumstances, or from any intention, good. Briefly, those intrinsically evil acts are expressed in the Ten Commandments; not to worship idols, not to curse God, not to kill the innocent, not to steal, not to commit adultery, not to bear false witness, not to covet. We cannot love any person, we cannot show friendship to anyone, where we collaborate with that person in what is intrinsically evil.

That is why the Church will not accept homosexual marriages, or sex outside of marriage. Similarly, an adulterous relationship cannot be true friendship, because the couple are having sex outside of their marriage relationship. It cannot be true friendship, because the two are co-operating in what is intrinsically an evil act, an act against what we saw as the 'natural law', the law written in our nature of right and wrong, expressed in the Ten Commandments, but interpreted by the Church down the centuries in its authentic moral teaching.

Q. But how can the Church tell me what love is, and what is good for me or for my friend? Is that not up to me, and my friend?

A. This is where we go back to Chapter 14, the first chapter on falling in love. We mentioned the influence of modern philosophy, particularly of Kant and of Romanticism. From the eighteenth-century Enlightenment and the nineteenth-century Romantic movement onwards, people tended to think that what was right was 'what I feel to be right'. It was not a question of what is objectively right and wrong.

Christian thinking has been influenced by a quite different philosophy, which harmonises much better with the Ten Commandments and with an objective law of right and wrong. Some historians consider that the scientific age began with Copernicus, Newton and the Renaissance in the sixteenth century. But a profounder look at history sees the scientific age beginning in the eleventh and twelfth centuries, with the founding of the great universities like Oxford, Cambridge and Paris by the Franciscan and Dominican friars.

We often think of the Middle Ages as a time of ignorance and superstition. That is to some extent a misreading of history, based upon the modern view of things post Renaissance and Reformation. In fact, the first centuries of the second millennium were the scenes of a great intellectual revival, both of philosophy and of science. That revolution was due to the importation of the works of the Greek philosopher Aristotle (384-322 BC). The manuscripts of Aristotle came to Europe via Arabic translations, in particular through the parts of Spain captured by the Moslems.

This caused a huge revolution in Christian thinking. Up to then, the main influence had been the philosophy of Plato (427-347 BC), who was a very spiritual thinker. For Plato, the 'real' world existed not here on earth, the mundane material world, but in a world of ideas, of which the world is only a pale reflection. Plato's thinking was the perfect underpinning of Christian thought in the early centuries. It made people think of the world to come as the true reality, to which we strive through this vale of tears, the imperfect world of sense experience.

Aristotle was an admirer and disciple of Plato, his master. But he rebelled against Plato's world of ideas. For Aristotle, the world of ideas was not in any other world, but was in the very essence of things. The ideas of the mind were what things actually are, in reality. When things act according to their nature, then they are acting correctly. Science, and philosophy, must find out what the essence of things is, to find out the laws which govern the created order. That is true for Aristotle both in philosophy and in science.

Catholic theology came very much under the influence of Aristotle through the teaching of St Thomas Aquinas, who called Aristotle 'the Philosopher'. It mattered nothing to Thomas that Aristotle lived long before the Christian era, and did not even know the Old Testament. What mattered for Thomas was that Aristotle saw the truth of reason. If things acted according to their nature, then they acted rightly. Aristotle did not know the law of God in the Bible. But, as St Paul said, Aristotle knew the law of God in his heart, in his being (Rom 2:15).

Thomas Aquinas used the ethics of Aristotle in particular. He realised that every situation could not be judged just by reading the Bible. The mind had to use its God-given reason to find out what was the right way to act. Recently,

Pope John Paul II, in his Encyclical letter *Fides et Ratio* (Faith and Reason), says that the reconciliation between faith and reason is Aquinas' greatest contribution for today:

> (43) A quite special place in this long development belongs to St Thomas, not only because of what he taught but also because of the dialogue which he undertook with the Arab and Jewish thought of his time. In an age when Christian thinkers were rediscovering the treasures of ancient philosophy, and more particularly of Aristotle, Thomas had the great merit of giving pride of place to the harmony which exists between faith and reason. Both the light of reason and the light of faith come from God, he argued; hence there can be no contradiction between them (44).
>
> More radically, Thomas recognised that nature, philosophy's proper concern, could contribute to the understanding of divine Revelation. Faith therefore has no fear of reason, but seeks it out and has trust in it. Just as grace builds on nature and brings it to fulfilment (45) so faith builds upon and perfects reason. Illumined by faith, reason is set free from the fragility and limitations deriving from the disobedience of sin and finds the strength required to rise to the knowledge of the Triune God.

For moral activity, therefore, according to the Catholic Church, we can trust our reason illuminated by faith. The Ten Commandments are themselves, as we have seen, the dictates of reason, of the Natural Law based upon God's eternal law. If we are to love truly, therefore, we must love what is right objectively, according to the good proposed by our reason. We cannot love a person and kill that person, even if that person feels it would be better to die. The good of that person's life is a fundamental value, given by God. If we love the person, we will love that good which is their life divinely given.

Similarly, we cannot love a person and act against the law of sexuality written into our being by God. That is what we have been demonstrating throughout this book. This means that a relationship which is adulterous cannot be right. A homosexual couple who love each other may not have sex together, because again that is against the law of union between man and woman written into our nature.

Q. But what happens when two people fall in love and their love leads to moral action contrary to God's law?

A. There are two possibilities: either stay together without sex, or run. This is one of the hardest decisions which human beings have to make. To love God and one's neighbour according to God's law is greater than any good on earth, even the good of human friendship.

The first option is to run away. This is not cowardice, but a decision against sin. It is more important for us to be right with God than any human friendship, however valuable, if that friendship inevitably leads to sin. 'Shun youthful passions and pursue righteousness, faith, love, and peace, along with those who call on the Lord from a pure heart' (2 Tim 2:22).

The word 'shun' is *pheug*, literally flee, run away from. The same word is used by Paul in his first letter to the Corinthians:

Shun immorality. Every other sin which a man commits is outside the body; but the immoral man sins against his own body. Do you not know that your body is a temple of the Holy Spirit within you, which you have from God? You are not your own; you were bought with a price. So glorify God in your body.

1 Corinthians 6:18-20, RSV

Paul is telling us to run away from immorality. That means to end a friendship if that friendship is clearly and inevitably leading to sin. There was a point in the story of *Falling in Love* where the two stars Robert de Niro and Meryl Streep, playing the role of two strangers already married falling in love, could have terminated the relationship. They did not. That relationship then went on to an emotional depth where neither could pull out, and it meant the end of their respective marriages.

Many of us know personally situations where this has occurred. May I give just one personal reminiscence. I was a newly ordained priest, out in Rome for further studies. I was given funds by my Archbishop to go to Germany as part of my biblical studies. I studied at Bonn University, living there for seven weeks on a German language course together with some one hundred and fifty mainly young students from all over the world.

I met an attractive French girl, who wanted me to develop a friendship with her. She said immediately that she thought that priests should marry. We found that we liked each other's company. It so happened that, on the Feast of the Assumption, 15 August, we all had a day off from studies. The organising group in the university suggested that all those who wished could visit the monastery Maria Laach, and have a pleasant day out on the Rhine. She suggested that the two of us went on a visit to the city of Aachen.

I knew that if I went to Aachen with her, my celibate priesthood was seriously in danger. I could feel myself falling in love. I think she was too. By God's grace, I said 'no' and went with the others. Strangely enough, just before we left for the trip, two Italian students came up to me and asked me if it was true that I was a Catholic priest. When I pleaded guilty to this, they asked me if I would say Mass during the trip. On their request, the authorities contacted a parish on the way, and I celebrated Mass on the Feast of the Assumption, with nearly one hundred students voluntarily present! I had found my family in the community of God's people, the Church, miles away from my home.

A much more dramatic illustration of the right kind of

running away is described in the magnificent film *Witness*. *Witness* is the story of an eight-year-old Amish boy, who, travelling with his mother (Kelly McGill) to visit their relative in the big city, runs into trouble. The boy Samuel Lapp sees a murder while visiting the public toilet, although he is himself unobserved. The detective John Book (Harrison Ford) questions the boy, and while in the police station, Samuel sees a photograph of the one he saw murdering another man in the station toilet. Harrison Ford informs his chief, not realising that his chief is himself part of the conspiracy. Book escapes an attempt on his life, but is wounded. He drives the mother, Rachel, back to her religious community, and faints while there. He is nursed back to health by the young mother, who falls in love with him, and he with her. Book becomes part of the religious community, hiding from his pursuers.

One night, after a hard day's farming, John Book stands at the doorway, looking intently in at Rachel washing. There is a silent pause, while Rachel slightly turns her head to see him standing behind her. Her eyes are ablaze with passion. She says no word, only turns round to stand fully facing him, her eyes on fire with love, her hair wet with her ablutions, and her body naked to the waist.

A few seconds' pause, and Rachel realises that, however much he wants to, her lover will not take those steps forward, even though the same fire is in his eyes. She turns slowly round again, showing him her back, to continue her wash. Book returns to his bedroom.

Next morning, the camera shows Book going to the barn where Rachel is working. He calls out 'Rachel', and she turns to face him as the night before, now dressed in the modest garb of the Amish woman. 'If I had made love to you last night' he says, 'either I would have had to stay, or you would have had to leave with me.' Rachel is silent, turns back again to continue her work.

John Book realised the human reality. He had to escape, if he was truly to love Rachel.

Q. But is escape the only possibility? Cannot friendship develop and grow without sex?

A. Of course, it can. There are many examples of relationships which have an element of sexual desire, yet where the two concerned have developed friendship which is without sex.

There are many examples of such friendships, both heterosexual and homosexual. Particularly where priests are concerned, there is the danger of scandal, if, for instance a priest is seen too often with one particular woman, even if there is no sexual intercourse involved. Justice must be seen to be done as well as done. But there can be warm friendships which develop, particularly by letter or by the occasional meeting. The same applies to relationships outside of marriage. Where a marriage is secure, a friendship can develop outside of that marriage. But the general rule is, when in doubt, run!

Finally, it is important to emphasise that some of the best friendships we develop have nothing whatever to do with sex. There is no element whatsoever of 'falling in love'. Our best friends very often particularly if they are of the same sex, arouse no sexual interest in us, nor we in them. This needs to be stated in the modern world, where post-Freud we tend to think that everything in life must be in some way or other related to sex.

In the cinema, the best example I remember is in the film *Showgirls*, by no means family entertainment, but with a powerful story. The anti-heroine is a showgirl trying to make her way in show business. She thumbs a lift to Las Vegas, but finds that the man giving her a lift has stolen her case with all her possessions. She becomes a striptease dancer, and rises to the top of the Vegas pile. She has had a history of abuse, which gives at least some reason why she is following her present path.

Having spent her first night in Vegas having had everything stolen, Nomi Malone literally bumps into a girl,

Molly, who invites her to share her caravan. Nomi goes through all kinds of sexual relationships connected with her sleazy job. But the film shows her with only one kind of genuine love: with her friend Molly. Neither has any sexual attraction one to the other. They just enjoy each other's company, and want each other's good. The most delightful scene in the film to me is when Nomi goes out to buy a dress accompanied by Molly. Just two girls out shopping. That is a beautiful friendship. When Molly is raped by a visiting pop star, Nomi manages to get into his room and knocks him senseless. Nomi makes a tearful goodbye to Molly, and leaves Las Vegas no more wealthy but much more wise. Nomi had found the love of true friendship. That was worth a great deal.

17

Homosexuality

Q. Is not the Catholic Church homophobic, frightened of homosexuality? Does not the homosexual have the same rights as one who is heterosexual?

A. 'Homophobic' means 'fearing homosexuals'. The Catholic Church has no fear of homosexuals as persons. They are children of God equal to everyone else. But the Church does have fear of the spread of homosexual practice in our society, and opposes that spread with all its might. That is because the Church, faithful to its constant Tradition, considers that homosexual acts are gravely disordered morally, and a serious abuse of the sexual faculties created by God, for the purpose of the personal union between male and female in the lifelong partnership of marriage, to bring from that sexual union children into the world. Read again Genesis chapters 1 and 2, how the male and female union is part of the creative plan of God from the beginning, two in one flesh. That plan is contradicted by the homosexual union.

This is what the Catechism says concerning chastity and homosexuality:

> 2357 Homosexuality refers to relations between men or between women who experience an exclusive or

predominant sexual attraction toward persons of the same sex. It has taken a great variety of forms through the centuries and in different cultures. Its psychological genesis remains largely unexplained. Basing itself on Sacred Scripture, which presents homosexual acts as acts of grave depravity, tradition has always declared that 'homosexual acts are intrinsically disordered'. They are contrary to the natural law. They close the sexual act to the gift of life. They do not proceed from a genuine affective and sexual complementarity. Under no circumstances can they be approved.

2358 The number of men and women who have deep-seated homosexual tendencies is not negligible. They do not choose their homosexual condition; for most of them it is a trial. They must be accepted with respect, compassion and sensitivity. Every sign of unjust discrimination in their regard should be avoided. These persons are called to fulfil God's will in their lives and, if they are Christians, to unite to the sacrifice of the Lord's Cross the difficulties they may encounter from their condition.

2359 Homosexual persons are called to chastity. By the virtues of self mastery that teach them inner freedom, at times by the support of disinterested friendship, by prayer and sacramental grace, they can and should gradually and resolutely approach Christian perfection.

To emphasise the wrongness of homosexual acts, may I repeat the two principles of Catholic sexual ethics outlined in Chapter 11:

- **The procreative aspect** That the sexual organs are (apart from their waste-disposal function) given to us by God for the procreation of new life. Thus any act which actively deprives a conjugal act from being open to procreation is gravely wrong, and against God's law.

- **The unitive aspect** That the sexuality of human persons is male–female orientated. This is in order that the pleasure of male–female sexual union will aid the bonding of a permanent relationship between the man and the woman. Thus the offspring of this union, new human beings each with an immortal soul, will enjoy the stability of this permanent relationship in order to grow and themselves learn to love God and neighbour.

Homosexual practice is wrong ethically on both counts. In homosexual acts, the sexual organs are not orientated towards procreation, but to the pleasure which two people of the same sex, male or female, wish to obtain from their stimulation. Second, in homosexual acts, the sexual organs are not being used for union between male and female, that 'one flesh' which is the norm in Genesis 1, ordained by God, but for an unnatural sexual union between those of the same sex.

Q. But surely, some men and women are naturally homosexual rather than heterosexual?

A. There is a big debate among psychologists and biologists as to whether some people are by their physical constitution orientated towards homosexual acts rather than heterosexual acts. That may or may not be true. When the Church calls homosexual activity 'unnatural' we are speaking in an ethical sense, where the human will is involved in a human act. Homosexual acts are *per se* and objectively wrong. Therefore, even if a person should happen to have a biological tendency in a homosexual direction, that tendency cannot ethically translate into homosexual activity.

It would be similar, granted the wrongness of homosexual acts, if a person claimed they could steal because they had biological genes which made them have a burning desire to steal. Stealing is against the Ten Commandments, so cannot be ethically justified just because a person has a tendency to want to do it. In the same way, homosexual acts are against the sixth commandment. It is the orientation of the sex act as ordained by God which is being violated in a homosexual act. Therefore, any tendency in a homosexual direction must be controlled, and cannot be expressed in homosexual acts.

Q. But there are great male friendships in the Bible, such as that between David and Jonathan. Surely, these are not excluded?

A. Not at all. A person with homosexual tendencies may be able to develop better and more fruitful friendships with a person of the same sex. But, where David and Jonathan are concerned, we are not sure whether their friendship was in any way sexually orientated, or rather was just a deep friendship of two people of the same sex: 'When David had finished speaking to Saul, the soul of Jonathan was bound to the soul of David, and Jonathan loved him as his own soul. Saul took him that day and would not let him return to his father's house. Then Jonathan made a covenant with David, because he loved him as his own soul' (1 Sam 18:1-3).

The Bible commends this friendship. It would hardly do so if that friendship were including homosexual acts, which were abominated in Israelite society. Leviticus 18 relates certain laws regarding sexual relationships, e.g. forbidding the marriage of close relatives. But, when it comes to the question of homosexual acts, much stronger language is used: 'You shall not lie with a male as with a woman; it is an abomination' (Lev 18:22).

That same horror of homosexual acts we find in St Paul, in that text we have quoted from the letter to the Romans. Paul is echoing the whole Old Testament tradition when he condemns the homosexual behaviour of the pagans:

Therefore God gave them up in the lusts of their hearts to impurity, to the degrading of their bodies among themselves, because they exchanged the truth about God for a lie and worshiped and served the creature rather than the Creator, who is blessed forever! Amen. For this reason God gave them up to degrading passions. Their women exchanged natural intercourse for unnatural, and in the same way also the men, giving up natural intercourse with women, were consumed with passion for one another. Men committed shameless acts with men and received in their own persons the due penalty for their error. And since they did not see fit to acknowledge God, God gave them up to a debased mind and to things that should not be done.

Romans 1:24-28

Of course, this is a generalisation. Paul is not saying that all the Greeks were like this although the homosexual practices of Hellenistic warriors were well known, Alexander the Great for instance having young boys to give him pleasure. Paul is saying that, if belief in the true God is abandoned, then immoral practices result. It is not too far from the arguments we have been introducing in this book. If a true idea of God is known, then a right ethical conscience develops in society, even if not everyone lives up to the values affirmed. That is where the confessional comes in!

Q. But surely, many homosexuals are just the way they are through no fault of their own. How can they be penalised for something which is not their fault?

A. Many homosexually orientated persons are heroic in their attempts to live a chaste Christian life. They may fall into temptation time after time. Sexual temptations cling like a leech. Time after time they have found help in the confessional, with a firm but encouraging and gentle confessor. But the priest cannot condone homosexual conduct, because the Church has always condemned homosexual

172

activity as wrong. The priest, like Jesus with the woman taken in adultery, can only say, 'Go, and sin no more' (Jn 8:6b-11). The priest can counsel help towards holiness, in guiding the person with that problem to genuine friendship in life. The homosexually orientated person will sometimes have very special gifts, e.g. the musical genius of Tchaikovsky. These gifts should be encouraged, and the homosexually orientated person should not be the subject of discrimination.

But, by the same token, the homosexual has a potential to corrupt young people into an orientation which is not theirs except through habit. We have granted the possibility that some may have a biological tendency towards homosexuality, although that is far from being proved. What is much clearer is that some will become homosexual through decisions as to sexuality made under the influence of someone else. The one influencing has a great deal to answer for here. Jesus has very harsh words to say about those who corrupt others, particularly the young: 'Whoever causes one of these little ones who believe in me to sin, it would be better for him to have a great millstone fastened round his neck and to be drowned in the depth of the sea' (Mt 18:6, RSV).

Likewise, modern society and commercial interests, which encourage gay practice by implicit and even explicit approval, have much to answer for here. The homosexual has the serious duty not to encourage others in that direction. Although, we must hasten to add here, many homosexuals, particularly those who are trying daily to live a chaste Christian life, would be revolted by the whole idea of leading someone else into sin.

Q. Why has child abuse come so much to the fore recently? Even some priests seem to have been involved?

A. It is right to link paedophilia with homosexuality, because often sexual acts with children are homosexual rather than heterosexual. It is a paradox again with our society that the age of homosexual consent has been lowered to sixteen. Therefore, a young teenager of sixteen can be corrupted by an older homosexual man or woman. But society has developed an increasing fear of paedophilia. This is not entirely misplaced, because there is a vast slave trade using children for sex, particularly in South East Asia; and everything must be done to stop this horrible practice.

But the lack of a sound sexual ethic makes modern anti-paedophilia seem more like panic. Again, with Catholic sexual ethics, it is clear why paedophilia is morally very wicked. The sex act is for adults only, male and female joined in marriage, precisely for the reasons we have been outlining in this book. Thus 'under-age' sex, and abuse of children by adults, is also seriously wrong, again because paedophilia or under-age sex fails to rise to the ethical norm of being procreative and unitive. But once this procreative and unitive principle is abandoned, there is no reason ethically why children should not enjoy sex like everyone else, or, if they can be persuaded to, enjoy sex with adults. Thus again it is clear that traditional Catholic ethics is the only rational protection for our vulnerable young, as providing the only sound sexual ethic which gives reasons against paedophilia.

It is particularly tragic when priests are involved, particularly because they are in a position of trust with the young. It is no consolation that the proportion of priests involved in child abuse is so tiny. In one or two cases, it seems that the priest lived with large numbers of boys. Again, a priest in this situation should either not have been ordained at all, or else have been posted to a situation where there was less temptation. In the Church today, there are also more structures of support for priests with this particular tendency, and recognition of the danger.

18

Masturbation

Q. Why is masturbation wrong?

A. First and foremost, because masturbation falls short of a genuine sexual relationship, which is of male and female spouses within a lifelong loving commitment.

> 2352 By *masturbation* is to be understood the deliberate stimulation of the genital organs in order to derive sexual pleasure. 'Both the Magisterium of the Church, in the course of a constant tradition, and the moral sense of the faithful have been in no doubt and have firmly maintained that masturbation is an intrinsically and gravely disordered action.' 'The deliberate use of the sexual faculty, for whatever reason, outside of marriage is essentially contrary to its purpose.' For here sexual pleasure is sought outside of 'the sexual relationship which is demanded by the moral order and in which the total meaning of mutual self-giving and human procreation in the context of true love is achieved.'

Q. OK, theoretically you may be right. But, for instance, teenagers often masturbate simply to experiment. And sometimes there is a 'wet dream' during

sleep. Finally, how often do people get into the habit of what used to be called 'self-abuse'? Surely, to give in under temptation, particularly last thing at night, in these circumstances cannot be considered a serious sin?

A. Fair questions. There are many instances in which masturbation, for one reason or another, is not a mortal sin. This is especially the case with the 'solitary act', where the full knowledge and consent which are required by a mortal sin (see Chapter 10, on forgiveness and responsibility) are not in evidence. We repeat the relevant and vital reference to the Catechism:

> 1859 Mortal sin requires *full knowledge and complete consent*. It presupposes knowledge of the sinful character of the act, of its opposition to God's law. It also implies a consent sufficiently deliberate to be a personal choice. Feigned ignorance and hardness of heart do not diminish, but rather increase, the voluntary character of a sin.

> 1860 *Unintentional ignorance* can diminish or even remove the imputability of a grave offence. But no one is deemed to be ignorant of the principles of the moral law, which are written in the conscience of every man. The promptings of feelings and passions can also diminish the voluntary and free character of the offence, as can external pressures or pathological disorders. Sin committed through malice, by deliberate choice of evil, is the gravest.

It is very rare that an act of masturbation is committed through malice. Rather, very often it is an act of weakness. It is not even a sin at all if the emission of semen takes place during sleep. That is obvious. But often an act of masturbation will take place in the twilight zone between sleeping and waking, where the person is not fully awake and therefore fully responsible. That is why a priest in the confessional is always very gentle and lenient regarding the confession of 'acts of impurity with myself', the confessional jargon to express the confession of masturbation.

The Catechism is very careful explicitly to mention, the possibility of the diminishment of responsibility regarding acts of masturbation. It is almost falling over backwards to ensure that unjustified feelings of guilt are not aroused in those who read the Catechism at this point:

> 2352 cont. To form an equitable judgement about the subjects' moral responsibility and to guide pastoral action, one must take into account the affective immaturity, force of acquired habit, conditions of anxiety or other psychological or social factors that lessen or even extenuate moral culpability.

Masturbation is a particular problem of a tense and egocentric twentieth century. Even the Kantian philosophy we have mentioned, where the mind reflects on itself rather than on considering an objective world in reality, may have played its part. No doubt, like every other sexual sin, masturbation took place in every age. But it does seem that, for instance, in the Middle Ages, it was not nearly so common as today (as also regarding suicide, which was little known in the Middle Ages). Surprisingly to us, a stricter penance was imposed for masturbation than for fornication in the mediaeval confessional guidebooks! The logic behind this was that masturbation was more unnatural than fornication. Fornication was at least a sexual act performed in the right way, even if it was the wrong male and female doing it. But masturbation was misusing an act which was designed by God for interpersonal communion to be used purely for solitary pleasure. The fact that masturbation was considered so seriously wrong in ancient times would seem to suggest that it was considered easier to avoid than it would be today.

The priest, therefore, is very lenient regarding masturbation in this day and age. He is a loving Christ welcoming the weak sinner back to full communion. But the Church will still not say that masturbation is morally right, but rather that it is *per se malum*, of itself evil, and can never be justified objectively. Thus it is wrong for a person to masturbate deliberately even for medical purposes. We cannot do evil that good may result.

Also, while young people in particular are vulnerable to begin the habit of masturbation, and cannot be held fully responsible always, yet there is always a natural human awareness that masturbation is at least hardly a good activity. Rather it is a degrading of the sexual act, turning what should be an act of male/female communion open to life into a solitary act of pleasure. As we have already quoted from the Catechism:

> 1860 cont. But no one is deemed to be ignorant of the principles of the moral law, which are written in the conscience of every man.

There is an awareness deep down in the human psyche that masturbation is by no means a praiseworthy act. Even the football crowds insult the referee by shouting out, 'The referee's a w...er'. Any Christian who genuinely repents and wishes to begin a new life in Christ will naturally wish to shake the habit of masturbation. This will lead to the control of desires and the opening of the heart to genuine love for others and for God.

Q. Why is the habit of masturbation so difficult to stop?

A. But – and this is the experience of confessors over the centuries – the habit of masturbation clings like a leech. Giving up smoking is much easier in comparison. The reason for sexual sin of any kind being habit-forming is precisely because it is a deeply personal act. Smoking only affects the body and its motor reactions. Sexual activity of every kind affects the human mind and heart as well as the body.

Masturbation could take many years, even a lifetime, to conquer. The well-known story of the man going to confession and saying, 'Well, Father, same old sins' to which the priest replies, 'No problem, same old absolution,' could well apply, among many sins, to masturbation.

But the struggle against temptation is worth it even if we sometimes, even often, lose. At least failure makes us humble, realising our human weakness. All the time, even in the midst of failure, the Spirit of God is working in the human heart, leading towards holiness.

We know that all things work together for good for those who love God, who are called according to his purpose. For those whom he foreknew he also predestined to be conformed to the image of his Son, in order that he might be the firstborn within a large family. And those whom he predestined he also called; and those whom he called he also justified; and those whom he justified he also glorified.

What then are we to say about these things? If God is for us, who is against us? He who did not withhold his own Son, but gave him up for all of us, will he not with him also give us everything else? Who will bring any charge against God's elect? It is God who justifies. Who is to condemn? It is Christ Jesus, who died, yes, who was raised, who is at the right hand of God, who indeed intercedes for us. Who will separate us from the love of Christ? Will hardship, or distress, or persecution, or famine, or nakedness, or peril, or sword? As it is written, 'For your sake,we are being killed all day long; we are accounted as sheep to be slaughtered.' No, in all these things we are more than conquerors through him who loved us. For I am convinced that neither death, nor life, nor angels, nor rulers, nor things present, nor things to come, nor powers,nor height, nor depth, nor anything else in all creation, will be able to separate us from the love of God in Christ Jesus our Lord.

Romans 8:28-39

I have quoted this passage from Romans because it is Paul at his best. Each Christian is called to the life of grace, and has the Holy Spirit poured into their heart. The very one who accuses us of sin is the same one who forgives us – even more, who has died to save us. Anyone who is truly sorry for sin will not only be forgiven, but will grow in the love of Christ. The Christian virtues will grow by the very fact of daily trial and temptation, even when we fall into sin. Even our sins work together for good to those who love God, because they make us realise our human weakness and drive us back more and more to dependence on God.

Christian faith tells us that the worst sin of all is pride. A person who is worried by sexual temptation, and might even frequently fall into sin, at least is not tempted to presumption and pride! Provided that that person is genuinely trying to become more holy day by day, the love of God in Jesus Christ is more than capable of coping with our sins. Day by day, the habit of virtue is gradually replacing the habit of sin. The virtues of hope and of fortitude are especially potent in the struggle against sin. We are promised by God himself that, if we co-operate with God's grace, we will win the daily battle against sin, because we have the life of grace in us:

1830 The moral life of Christians is sustained by the gifts of the Holy Spirit. These are permanent dispositions which make man docile in following the promptings of the Holy Spirit.

1831 The seven *gifts* of the Holy Spirit are wisdom, understanding, counsel, fortitude, knowledge, piety and fear of the Lord. They belong in their fullness to Christ,

Son of David. They complete and perfect the virtues of those who receive them. They make the faithful docile in readily obeying divine inspirations.

> Let your good spirit lead me on a level path.
>
> Psalm 143:10
>
> For all who are led by the Spirit of God are sons of God... If children, then heirs, heirs of God and fellow heirs with Christ.
>
> Romans 8:14, 17

1832 The fruits of the Spirit are perfections that the Holy Spirit forms in us as the first fruits of eternal glory. The tradition of the Church lists twelve of them: 'charity, joy, peace, patience, kindness, goodness, generosity, gentleness, faithfulness, modesty, self-control, chastity' (Gal 5:22-3).

Q. How often should one go to confession?

A. First of all, it must be said that it takes courage to go to confession to confess sexual sins. This means that the very act of going to confession is itself an act of the virtue of courage, or fortitude, which is so necessary in the Christian life. It took courage, real guts, for the Prodigal Son to go back to his father and confess that he had squandered his inheritance:

> I will get up and go to my father, and I will say to him, 'Father, I have sinned against heaven and before you; I am no longer worthy to be called your son; treat me like one of your hired hands.' So he set off and went to his father. But while he was still far off, his father saw him and was filled with compassion; he ran and put his arms around him and kissed him. Then the son said to him, 'Father, I have sinned against heaven and before you; I am no longer worthy to be called your son.'
>
> Luke 15:18-21

Above all, the sinner has the help of the Holy Spirit in the Sacrament of Penance. Regarding masturbation, as we have said, as regarding many other kinds of sexual sin, very frequently that full co-operation which makes a mortal sin is not verified. It may not even be a sin at all, as we have said above, if it was involuntary. The most important advice to be given is therefore not to panic, but to go to confession at the earliest reasonable opportunity, as much for consolation and help as for the forgiveness of Christ in the sacrament. If it is not possible to go to confession before the next Mass, then remember that sin can be forgiven by a personal act of contrition; then confession at the next reasonable opportunity, say within a week or two. For centuries, Catholics have found the strength and consolation in the Sacrament of Penance for growth in daily virtue, particularly regarding those sins which above all indicate our human weakness. This is what the Catechism says about the sacrament of confession:

> 1470 In this sacrament, the sinner, placing himself before the merciful judgement of God, *anticipates* in a certain way *the judgement* to which he will be subjected at the end of his earthly life. For it is now, in this life, that we are offered the choice between life and death, and it is only by the road of conversion that we can enter the Kingdom, from which one is excluded by grave sin. In converting to Christ through penance and faith, the sinner passes from death to life and 'does not come into judgement' (Jn 5:24).

Keep trying! Never despair!

19

Pornography or naked beauty?

Q. You are on a losing wicket regarding pornography, surely. As time goes on, advertising, films, theatre become more and more sexually explicit. Are you not just fighting a rearguard action here?

A. Certainly, since the sixties and the so-called 'sexual revolution', sexually explicit pictures and scenes have become more and more commonplace. The stout fight put up in the sixties by Mary Whitehouse – a lady with much courage and much to be admired rather than abused, as she was – has in no way stemmed the pornographic tide. Rather, still another entirely new media in addition to television and the home video industry, the computer internet, is providing a yet more efficient means of the mass communication of erotic stimulation of all kinds, even the most lurid, such as sado-masochism and child pornography.

Furthermore, you guessed right. The Church unequivocally condemns pornography as degrading both for those who watch and for those who participate:

> 2354 *Pornography* consists in removing real or simulated sexual acts from the intimacy of the partners, in order to display them deliberately to third parties. It

offends against chastity because it perverts the conjugal act, the intimate giving of spouses to each other. It does grave injury to the dignity of its participants (actors, vendors, the public), since each one becomes an object of base pleasure and illicit profit for others. It immerses all who are involved in the illusion of a fantasy world. It is a grave offence. Civil authorities should prevent the production and distribution of pornographic materials.

Even in this promiscuous age, there is some agreement here in society. All agree that child pornography and more extreme forms of sado-masochism (the horrific so-called 'snuff movies', where actual torture and even death is inflicted on the victims of a crime) must be stamped out by law.

What is not so clear is why pornography of any kind is wrong. People just react to feelings in condemning child pornography and sado-masochism. But, on late night television, there is encouragement of sex purely for pleasure, apparently without bounds. For instance, many homosexual persons, and indeed heterosexual persons, will have a strong sexual urge to have under-age sex. Why is it wrong? The sex industry gives us no answers here, except to warn us that it is illegal. Again, the answer comes from the Church, the true defender against such moral anarchy. The Catholic Catechism insists that when the sex act is isolated from its true context within the union of love and life in permanent marriage, then it is clearly wrong to display such a sex act to stimulate sexual activity of any kind outside marriage.

As a counter to pornography, the Church encourages modesty, a much ridiculed concept today. Yet again, even the modern world on occasions encourages modesty. An advertisement showing a small boy dressed only in his underpants was made to be withdrawn by the advertising company because of possible stimulation towards child pornography. The world admits the principle at least that modesty is sometimes a virtue. The Catechism gives us a clear definition of it:

2521 Purity requires modesty, an integral part of temperance. Modesty protects the intimate centre of the person. It means refusing to unveil what should remain hidden. It is ordered to chastity to whose sensitivity it bears witness. It guides how one looks at others and behaves toward them in conformity with the dignity of persons and their solidarity.

2522 Modesty protects the mystery of persons and their love. It encourages patience and moderation in loving relationships; it requires that the conditions for the definitive giving and commitment of man and woman to one another be fulfilled. Modesty is decency. It inspires one's choice of clothing. It keeps silence or reserve where there is evident risk of unhealthy curiosity. It is discreet.

2523 There is a modesty of the feelings as well as of the body. It protests, for example, against the voyeuristic explorations of the human body in certain advertisements, or against the solicitations of certain media that go too far in the exhibition of intimate things. Modesty inspires a way of life which makes it possible to resist the allurements of fashion and the pressures of prevailing ideologies.

2524 The forms taken by modesty vary from one culture to another. Everywhere, however, modesty exists as an intuition of the spiritual dignity proper to man. It is born with the awakening consciousness of being a subject.

Teaching modesty to children and adolescents means awakening in them respect for the human person.

Q. But surely, the display of the naked body is not always wrong?

A. Indeed not. Earlier, we spoke about the doctrine of Original Sin. In the primitive story in Genesis, the first man and woman Adam and Eve were, we are told, 'naked and not ashamed' (Gen 2:25). The shame resultant upon nakedness results from fear of the lust of the party looking on, or the sense of dominance of viewing an exposed part which is again only the result of a disordered nature. In a normal innocent state of affairs, there should be no shame in nakedness because there is no fear of lust or of dominance.

All acknowledge the acceptability of viewing the naked body in the context of medical or surgical treatment, although even here the medical profession rightly preserves the dignity of the patient by practising modesty in its medical examinations and hospital procedures, avoiding unnecessary exposure of the body. Particularly in old people's homes, where helpless old people live together, it is easy for a harassed staff to cause some loss of dignity among the senior residents by not observing proper decency in dressing and undressing patients. Remarks like 'Don't worry, dear, we've all seen it before' or 'You won't mind, love, you're past all that kind of thing now', offend human dignity and humiliate the helpless. A patient would not be publicly undressed in a hospital; then why in a poor persons' home?

More controversial is the use of nudity in art. This is well established, even in religious paintings and sculpture. Michaelangelo painted a full frontal naked Adam on the ceiling of the pope's own Sistine Chapel, which seems never to have caused scandal even in a sacred place. Most of us saw our first naked adults on primary school visits to art galleries. How we all sniggered, and were rebuked by our teachers

As the Catechism quotation above reminds us, the, standards of modesty vary from culture to culture. In a former age, a woman would have been considered daring to expose her ankle. In Moslem countries, women are not permitted to show their faces in public, to preserve modesty. Yet those of us who have visited a crowded continental topless beach have no doubt been surprised at the apparent lack of voyeurism. Hundreds of naked female bosoms seem to cause no more scandal than the breasts of the males on view.

There may be one important positive contribution from the present sexually liberated age. We may be able more and more genuinely to appreciate the beauty of the naked human body. It is a penalty of Original Sin that we are not able to appreciate the full beauty of the naked body, but incline towards inordinate lust of that body; wishing to possess it in a way which is not right. But that lust is only in our mind. If purified, we could really appreciate the beauty of the greatest creation of God, the human body destined not only for physical life but spiritual life.

St Paul, or his disciple, writes to Titus, 'To the pure all things are pure, but to the corrupt and unbelieving nothing is pure. Their very minds and consciences are corrupted' (Tit 1:15). If a person is truly pure, then that person can look without lust on God's creation, and admire its beauty without inordinately desiring it.

Beauty is related to life. The beauty of a flower is designed by God to attract the attentions of the bee: sexual attentions, no less. Without having the physical desires of the bee, the desire to suck the pollen, we human beings are able nevertheless to appreciate the beauty of that flower, its beauty first and foremost designed to arouse the hunger of the bee. Likewise, the beauty of the woman, her sexual parts – her breasts, her navel, her vagina – are designed by the Creator to attract the love of a man who will join that woman in permanent union of love to enable the human family to grow. Without the sexual desire, that woman's naked beauty still can be appreciated precisely as beauty. The same applies to the naked beauty of the man, his strong thighs and shoulders, his testicles and penis, designed by the Creator to attract the woman. We can view the human body as a beautiful object of creation. That does not mean that there is no erotic element included even in an innocent

187

appreciation of naked beauty. But, in a pure individual, that desire is controlled and purified into the love of the beautiful form itself as a creation of a loving God.

We are told in the book of Genesis that after God had created the world, the sea, the fishes in the sea, the animals, and finally the man and the woman 'God saw everything that he had made, and indeed, it was very good. And there was evening and there was morning, the sixth day'(Gen 1:31). To see naked beauty in purity is to see the human body with the pleasure that God has when he sees his own creation.

Q. But when is it 'pornography' and when is it 'beauty' and 'art'?

A. This is a very difficult question, and cannot be answered absolutely. That is why the film censor's job is so difficult, deciding what is acceptable for public viewing and what is not. It is easy to pretend that pornography is 'art'. It is a joke in the barrack room. The soldiers have cut out pin-ups from the recent *Playboy* magazine. 'It is art', they tell each other. They are joking, of course.

Partly, it is a question of the 'eye of the beholder'. What is naked beauty to one pair of eyes could easily be lustful desire on the part of another. But we can all work towards a more innocent, and therefore more human, appreciation of the naked body. This will help us to conquer inordinate desires, certainly better than repressing those desires, or adopting puritan attitude to sex, running away from any consideration of it. We have seen earlier where it might be necessary for an individual to run away from a situation where they are becoming embroiled in a relationship which is wrong. Sometimes, it is right to run. But we cannot run away all the time from ourselves, and from our own desires. These must be faced and controlled. An ability to view nakedness without lust could be a very positive way of progressing in chastity.

But how can we move from lust to appreciation of beauty? First, we consider what beauty precisely is. In our second chapter, we saw how we all have a desire within us for the ultimate good, which is God. That good is not simply something which our senses like. It is a choice of our will, of our minds. We choose the good by a voluntary act. The Ten Commandments tell us the evil which is to be avoided. We choose the opposite good to the evil condemned in the commandments: piety, love of parents, fidelity in marriage, justice and truth in our relationships, rejoicing when someone else is successful. We can choose these 'goods'. That again is what distinguishes us from the animals, who can only react with their senses. We can choose either the good or the evil.

What, then, is the beautiful? Aquinas in his analysis tells us that the beautiful is closely related to the good which we choose:

> The beautiful and the good are the same thing in a given subject, because they are based upon the same thing, namely upon the form: and for this reason, the good is praised as the beautiful. But there is a difference. For the good properly is related to the appetite; for it is the good which everything desires. For this reason, the good can be seen under the aspect of a final purpose; for our appetite is like a certain motive towards an end. Now, what is beautiful relates to our cognitive powers. What is said to be beautiful is what pleases our sight. Therefore, what is beautiful consists of due proportion; because our senses delight in things which are of due proportion, that is to say in things similar to ourselves.
>
> *Summa Theologiae* 1, q.5, a.4, ad.1

Aquinas here uses terms in a slightly different way than we would. When he says that our 'appetite' desires the 'good', he is not simply referring to our senses. We usually refer to the 'appetite' as related to food. But Aquinas here uses 'appetite' as the desire within us to value what we choose voluntarily. For him, everything begins with the senses, but then goes beyond it. The good which we perceive with our senses inclines us to choose what is good.

For Aquinas, the beautiful is interchangeable with the good. The beautiful is the good which we perceive with our senses; we are attracted to it because it is like us, and we then appreciate it for its due proportion. To appreciate the naked form of the body, therefore, is to choose it as the good, our eyes having been attracted to it by its due proportion. But it then becomes a deliberate and voluntary choice, to appreciate its due proportion as the good desired by our wills, and not simply by our senses. That is to appreciate its 'integrity, due proportion, and clarity', Aquinas' definition of the beautiful.

That is the way in which the artist appreciates every form, including the form of the naked body. To appreciate the nude body without lust can be truly a liberating experience which helps towards self-control and so to chastity.

Q. What of simulated sex acts performed in public?

A. This is a different matter. If the naked form is immobile, there is a real possibility that we can view that body as beautiful in form, without lust, although even here, as we all realise, we must beware of self-deception.

However, if two naked bodies are simulating the sex act, it is difficult to see how this could not be primarily an act which degrades not only the sex act itself, but also the couple taking part in it, and the viewing public.

The quotation from the *Catechism of the Catholic Church* refers also to the insult which the simulated act delivers to the intimacy of the sex act.

> 2354 Pornography consists in removing real or simulated sexual acts from the intimacy of the partners, in order to display them deliberately to third parties. It

offends against chastity because it perverts the conjugal act, the intimate giving of spouses to each other.

We mentioned earlier the fact that, in a state of innocence, nudity bears no shame because of the absence of Original Sin. In heaven, we would admire the beauty of the naked body without lusting after it. However, concerning the sex act, even in a state of innocence the viewing of the sex act might not be permissible, because the sex act is so intimate to the two lovers themselves. It is in its essence an exclusive act between two people who love each other and wish to share their intimacy with each other. It even might look somewhat ridiculous to those watching who do not share that intimacy. In truly 'knowing' each other, the couple wish to have intimate space to themselves. That is why pornographic sexual activity, just for the pleasure of those watching, is so degrading.

20

Male and female: image of God

Q. Why did God make us male and female?

A. The simple answer was given earlier: that God created us male and female to enable procreation of new human life to be the result on the human level of an intimate partnership between one man and one woman, two in one flesh. That was, in God's plan, to foster the union of male/female love in the world, the child of that loving union to grow up in a tiny community of faithful love, the family. No organisation has promoted that marriage union, and promoted it more successfully despite many failures, than the Church.

But there is a much more profound answer as to why God made us male and female, and more of a mystery:

Then God said, 'Let us make humankind in our image, according to our likeness; and let them have dominion over the fish of the sea, and over the birds of the air, and over the cattle, and over all the wild animals of the earth, and over every creeping thing that creeps upon the earth.' So God created humankind in his image, in the image of God he created them; male and female he created them. God blessed them, and God said to them, 'Be fruitful and multiply, and fill the earth and subdue it; and have dominion over the fish of the sea and over the birds of the air and over every living thing that moves upon the earth.'

Genesis 1:26-28

For this author of the book of Genesis, many centuries before Christ, the male and the female human beings were, precisely as male and female, in the image of God. What does that mean?

First of all, not every creature was made in God's image. Not the creatures, the animals, which God created before he created humankind. Only man and woman, who as we say have an immortal soul specially created by God, are in his image. Our yearning for the infinite God arises itself from our intellect which shares in God's mind.

The teaching of the Catholic Church has long recognised that our immortal soul is the image of God:

> 33 The *human person*: With his openness to truth and beauty, his sense of moral goodness, his freedom and the voice of his conscience, with his longings for the infinite and for happiness, man questions himself about God's existence. In all this he discerns signs of his spiritual soul. The soul, the 'seed of eternity we bear in ourselves, irreducible to the merely material', can have its origin only in God.

But the Church has come more and more to realise that not only the human individual is made in God's image and likeness with its immortal soul; but also that the union of man and woman in the sex act is itself the image of God. The Catechism again:

> 2335 Each of the two sexes is an image of the power and tenderness of God, with equal dignity though in a different way. The *union of man and woman* in marriage is a way of imitating in the flesh the Creator's generosity

and fecundity: 'Therefore a man leaves his father and his mother and cleaves to his wife, and they become one flesh.' All human generations proceed from this union.

Q. But how are male and female in the image of God?

A. In the sex act, the male sperm fertilises the female ovum. The 'power' is present in the active male sperm, the 'tenderness' is in the soft female womb which forms a home for the growing tiny embryo.' And this union, unlike the birth of animals even by a similar sexual process, is especially one where God is involved: 'Now the man knew his wife Eve, and she conceived and bore Cain, saying, "I have produced a man with the help of the LORD"' (Gen 4:1). Woman is therefore not only a child-bearer, but is a 'God-bearer', giving birth to a little child who is also in God's image and likeness.

Modern biology sees this description as somewhat primitive and misleading. It will tell us that there is as much creative power in the body of the female as in the male seed being injected.

But as an *image*, this seems not unreasonable. Certainly, in Christian tradition, God is mainly called Father, indeed the 'Father Omnipotent', all-powerful. The Mother is mainly the Church, or Mary the 'God-bearer', Mother of God as she is called in Catholic faith. Even in primitive mythology, God is male, and the woman is Mother Earth, who receives the seed and gives birth in the 'soil' of her womb. We see this kind of imagery in the Epistle to the Ephesians:

Husbands, love your wives, just as Christ loved the church and gave himself up for her, in order to make her holy by cleansing her with the washing of water by the word, so as to present the church to himself in splendour, without a spot or wrinkle or anything of the kind – yes, so that she may be holy and without blemish.
Ephesians 5:25-27

I realise that an extreme feminism will be angry at my pursuing these analogies. But it does seem to me that we must hold on to the traditional imagery of the Church. The Church, has never permitted female images of God. The female as image of God is 'God bearer', a creature who is specially chosen to bring forth God. The male is the image of the Creator God, who sows the seed in the chosen woman to bring forth a new being in God's image. That again is why when God became incarnate in Jesus, it was more appropriate that he should have been incarnate as a male rather than as a female. Jesus said, 'Whoever has seen me has seen the Father' (Jn 14:9). Christ is the image not of the God-bearer but of God the Father, the Creator who sows the seed of the Word first in Mary his chosen Mother, and then in the Church through the Sacraments. That may also be seen as one of the reasons why it is more appropriate for males to be priests than females: because Christ as male is the Head of the Church, and the priest at Mass represents Christ as Head.

The theologian Hans Urs von Balthasar argues that 'the creature can only be secondary, responsive, "feminine" vis-a-vis God' (H.U. Von Balthasar, *Theodrama: Theological Dramatic Theory. II. Dramatis Personae: Persons in Christ*, translated by Graham Harrison, San Francisco, Ignatius Press, 1992, p. 287). The concept of the female always implies that a creative act has already taken place in her, in order for her to give birth to God present in the new human soul. By the same token, the female is a more perfect creature, precisely because she is more creaturely in receiving the creative seed of God.

Q. But does not this argue to the inherent superiority of male over female?

A. Some theologians – male of course! – have argued this in the past. But again, we are only talking of images. Male and female are equal in dignity as human, as the Catechism puts it. Also, it seems to me, God has used his own particular sense of humour to ensure that we males do not get ideas beyond our station!

What distinguishes us from the female creature? What physical part of the male signifies that creative act which makes a man the symbol of the creative Fatherhood of God? A tube a few inches long and a sack holding two small spherical objects. A wonderful creation indeed, as all our bodies, complex beyond measure, but still just a little bit ridiculous. The Wife of Bath, whom we have already mentioned, in Chaucer's *Canterbury Tales* refers to man's 'silly instrument'. She ought to know. She gave birth to many children, and survived the death of more than one husband!

We all remember those saucy postcards for sale on our seaside holiday. A little girl is looking down at her baby brother sitting in the bath. She looks up and tells her mother, 'Mummy, little Johnny has a thorn between his legs.' In similar vein, in the film *Carry on Nurse*, a male patient (played by Kenneth Connor) is being admitted into the ward, and prepared for bed by the nurses. He is somewhat embarrassed at the prospect of being undressed by two attractive young females. But, reluctantly, he is rapidly divested of his trousers and put into his pyjamas, finding himself tucked up in bed before he can protest effectively. 'Now, Mr Smith,' says the staff nurse 'what a fuss over such a little thing.'

God does have a creative sense of humour, I am sure. Even that has a purpose: to make us look beyond male and female creation, even beyond marriage and human relationships, to what the images represent, the power and tenderness of God, who invites us to friendship with him, on this earth and for eternity. No doubt, God's greatest creation was woman; not only her physical beauty, but the beauty of her tender love. This to me has best been expressed, not in the Bible nor in the Catechism, but the lovely poem of the so-called Bad Lord Byron. He could not have been completely bad if he could write a poem like

'She walks in beauty' (John Stallworthy, (ed.) *The Penguin Book of Love Poetry*, Penguin Books, London, 1976).

> She walks in beauty, like the night
> Of cloudless climes and starry skies,
> And all that's best of dark and bright
> Meet in her aspect and her eyes
> Thus mellowed to that tender light
> Which heaven to gaudy day denies.
>
> One shade the more, one ray the less
> Had half impaired the nameless grace
> Which waves in every raven tress
> Or softly lightens o'er her face
> Where thoughts serenely sweet express
> How pure, how dear their dwelling place.
>
> And on that cheek, and o'er that brow
> So soft, so calm, yet eloquent,
> The smiles that win, the tints that glow
> But tell of days in goodness spent
> A mind at peace with all below
> A heart whose love is innocent.

This poem is a perfect expression of the Catholic devotion to Mary. Mary, Mother of Jesus, Mother of God, God-bearer, is only a creature, a feminine creature. The light shining from her is the light of the moon, not of the sun, which is Christ her Son, God become flesh in her womb. Yet her created beauty, her tender virtue, communicates that innocent love which we all seek from her Son. She has that love as his 'dwelling place'.

> Hail Mary, full of grace, the Lord is with thee.
> Blessed art thou among women, and blessed is the
> fruit of thy womb, Jesus.
> Holy Mary, Mother of God, pray for us sinners now
> and at the hour of our death. Amen.

St Maria Goretti

Maria Goretti was born in 1890 at Corinaldo, a village some thirty miles from Ancona, the daughter of a farm labourer, Luigi Goretti, and his wife Assunta Carlini. They had five other children, and in 1896 the family moved to Colle Gianturco, near Galiano, and later to Ferriere di Conca, not far from Nettuno in the Roman Campagna. Almost at once after settling down here, Luigi Goretti was stricken with malaria and died. His widow had to take up his work as best she could, but it was a hard struggle and every small coin and bit of food had to be looked at twice. Of all the children none was more cheerful and encouraging to her mother than Maria, commonly called Marietta.

On a hot afternoon in July 1902 Maria was sitting at the top of the stairs in the cottage, mending a shirt: she was not yet quite twelve years old. A cart stopped outside, and a neighbour, a young man of eighteen named Alexander, ran up the stairs. He beckoned Maria into an adjoining bedroom, she refused to go. Alexander seized hold of her, pulled her in, and shut the door.

Maria struggled and tried to call for help, but she was being half-strangled and could only protest hoarsely, gasping that she would be killed rather than submit; whereupon Alexander half pulled her dress from her body and began striking at her blindly with a long dagger. She sank to the floor, crying out that she was being killed, Alexander plunged the dagger into her back, and ran away.

An ambulance fetched Maria to hospital, where it was seen at once that she could not possibly live. Her last hours were most touching – her concern for where her mother was going to sleep, her forgiveness of her murderer (she disclosed that she had been going in fear of him, but did not like to say anything lest she cause trouble with his family), her childlike welcoming of the holy viaticum. Some twenty-four hours after the assault, Maria Goretti died. Her mother, the parish priest of Nettuno, a Spanish noblewoman and two nuns, had watched by her bed all night.

Alexander was sentenced to thirty years' penal servitude. He was unrepentant. Then one night he had a dream in which Maria Goretti appeared gathering flowers and offering them to him. From then on he was a changed man. At the end of twenty-seven years he was released, his first act when free was to visit Maria's mother to beg her forgiveness.

Meanwhile the memory of his victim had become more and more revered. On 27 April 1947, Maria Goretti was declared blessed by Pope Pius XII. When he afterwards appeared on the balcony of St Peter's he was accompanied by Maria's mother, Assunta Goretti, then eighty-two years old, together with two of Maria's sisters and a brother. Three years later the same pope canonized Maria Goretti in the piazza of St Peter's, before the biggest crowd ever assembled for a canonization. Her murderer was still alive.

Ed. Michael Walsh, *Butler's Lives of the Saints*,
concise edition, revised 1985, Tunbridge Wells,
Burns and Oates, pp. 206-7

The Office of Readings

A reading from the homily of Pope Pius XII for the canonization of St Maria Goretti:

Everyone knows how this defenceless girl had to resist a violent attack when a savage storm broke over her and threatened to destroy her purity. But faced with this crisis she was able to repeat the words of that golden book, *The Imitation of Christ*: 'Even if I am to experience grievous temptations I shall have no fear as long as I have your grace. This is my strength, this gives me help and direction. This is more powerful than any enemy.' Sustained by divine grace and the response of the firm resolution of her will, she laid down her life and preserved her glorious virginity.

In the humble life of this girl which we have sketched briefly we have an example not alone deserving the rewards of heaven but worthy of the admiration and respect of our present-day world. Let fathers and mothers try to bring up the children given them by God in a truly holy and steadfast manner and bring them up in the tenets of the Catholic faith, so that when their virtue is endangered they may, by the grace of God, emerge from the struggle unconquered, pure and unsullied.

Let those who are in the happy days of youth learn not to waste their energies on the transient empty pleasures of self-indulgence. Let them be on their guard against the temptation of sinful pleasures and the wretchedness of yielding to vice. Rather may they strive vigorously to form their character in the way of Christian living, hard and rough though the way may be. For this perfection can indeed be attained through personal determination, helped by the grace of God, prayer and perseverance.

Not all of us are called to undergo martyrdom, but we are all called to a life of Christian virtue. Now virtue demands courage. It may not reach the heights attained by this young girl. Nevertheless, it demands from us daily, assiduous, unremitting effort to our very last breath, and so it can be called a slow and continuous martyrdom. This is what our Lord Jesus Christ urges on us in his words: 'The Kingdom of Heaven suffers violence, and the violent bear it away.' Let this then be our goal, with God's grace to sustain us. May the holy virgin and martyr Maria Goretti strengthen our resolve. May she who now enjoys the eternal happiness of heaven obtain from our divine Saviour by her prayers the grace for each of us to imitate her example gladly, willingly and wholeheartedly.

Appendix

A brief introduction
to Natural Family Planning

What is Natural Family Planning?

Natural Family Planning (NFP) is quite simply using the natural signs of human fertility to understand the natural fertility cycle of a woman, and then using that understanding to plan a family. In using this understanding, it develops a couple's respect for fertility, and for each other, as they grow in knowledge of each other and of the gift of fertility.

NFP can be used either to plan pregnancy or to avoid it – it has an effectiveness level as high as artificial contraception, and it is safe to use with no unpleasant side effects. Because it is scientifically based on the natural signs of fertility, NFP can be used reliably by any fertile woman, regardless of cycle length, age or other factors. It can also be used while breastfeeding, and during times of changing fertility such as the pre-menopause.

The natural signs of fertility

There are various signs of fertility which can be observed by a woman to gain an understanding of her fertility patterns. The main signs are:

1. The mucus signs before and during the time of ovulation.

The mucus is an essential aid to fertility: without it conception would not take place. It is secreted at the cervix (the neck of the womb) and can be checked either at the cervix or externally. Many women are aware of it without knowing what it means, and learning to recognise it and understand what it is saying about your fertility is an easy step.

2. The small but measurable rise in basal body temperature which occurs after ovulation.

Using an ovulation thermometer, and taking the temperature at the same time every day (or at the same stage of the day for people on shift-work or with other unusual sleep patterns), you can make a chart of the daily temperatures and see when the rise takes place.

3. The changes in the cervix around ovulation.

The cervix itself can be checked to identify a series of changes relating to the different parts of the fertility cycle.

These signs can be used either individually – the Billings Method (also called the Ovulation Method), for example, relies upon the mucus sign alone – or together in a cross-checking way in the Symptothermal Method.

There are also secondary signs, such as ovulation pain and breast tenderness, which are often helpful.

Learning NFP

Whilst it is possible to learn NFP from a book, it is much better to be taught directly by a qualified teacher, or a proper self-study course backed up by contact with a teacher. If you do choose to teach yourself, you should always have your first few charts checked by someone with appropriate qualifications.

The Couple to Couple League (CCL) teaches the Symptothermal Method of NFP and covers the connection between breastfeeding and child spacing. CCL has teaching couples in many countries internationally and in various parts of the UK. CCL also provides a Home Study Course backed up by regular telephone or postal contact with teachers.

CCL in Britain can be contacted by telephone at 0115 925 9078 or by email at info@cclgb.org.uk

CCL's international headquarters in the USA can be contacted on +513 471 2000, or by email at ccli@ccli.org

WOOMB (The World Organisation Ovulation Method Billings) teaches the Billings Method of NFP, and also has teachers in many parts of the world and of the UK.
In Britain, telephone 02071793 0026. WOOMB's international office in Australia can be contacted on +61 3 9481 1722 or by email at enquiries@woomb.org